Advanced Course of an Embedded Systems Design

Dr.K. Naveen Karunya

Dr.R. Prakash Rao

Dr.S. Prabhakar Rao

Gorre Narsimhulu

Published by

BONFRING®
Intellectual Integrity

Advanced Course of an Embedded Systems Design

9 789387 862517 >

ISBN 978-93-87862-51-7

Authors

Dr.K. Naveen Karunya

Dr.R. Prakash Rao

Dr.S. Prabhakar Rao

Gorre Narsimhulu

Bonfring

309, 2nd Floor,

5th Street Extension, Gandhipuram,

Coimbatore-641 012.

Tamilnadu, India.

E-mail: info@bonfring.org

Website: www.bonfring.org

Phone: 0422 4213231

Preface

This book entitled **"Advanced Course of an Embedded Systems Design"** has been written in accordance with the syllabus prescribed by the 'JNTUH R13, R15 and R17' for the Third and Final Year, B.Tech & M.Tech students of Engineering colleges affiliated to JNTUH.

This book comprises of five chapters which covers Jawaharlal Nehru Technological University, Hyderabad syllabus. The main emphasis of the book is to explain in a simple manner, the logical concepts that will enable Even the beginners to understand them without difficulty.

Systematic care has been taken to support the topics with necessary illustrations and relevant diagrams to make learning much easier. It is believed that this book shall serve all the requirements of Final Year Engineering students.

It covers all the important questions that have appeared in the previous years of Jawaharlal Nehru Technological University, Hyderabad Examinations. Most of the topics covered well in advance of the updated Technologies.

Your suggestions are most welcome.

Dr.K. Naveen Karunya

Dr.R. Prakash Rao

Dr.S. Prabhakar Rao

Gorre Narsimhulu

Preface

Acknowledgement

We sincerely thank the Almighty GOD for being with us through all stages of the preparation of this book.

Firstly, we would like to express our sincere gratitude to **The Chairman T. Bala Reddy, St.Peters Engineering College** for the continuous support motivation, and immense knowledge.

Special Acknowledgement is due to our Secretary **T.V. Reddy, St.Peters Engineering College** for his continuous support for the successful completion of this book.

We thank **Dr.M. Narendra Kumar, Principal, St.Peters Engineering College** for his source of inspiration.

We thank our Friends and Colleagues for their encouragement and support in various stages of writing this book.

We express our sincere thanks to our publisher **VSRD Academic Publishing (A Division of Visual Soft India Private Limited)**, for their help and co-operation in publishing this book.

Dr.K. Naveen Karunya

Dr.R. Prakash Rao

Dr.S. Prabhakar Rao

Gorre Narsimhulu

Acknowledgement

Authors Profile

Dr.K. Naveen Karunya currently working as Professor in the Department of ECE, St. Peter's Engineering College affiliated to Jawaharlal Nehru Technological University (JNTUH), Hyderabad. He has completed Ph.D research in Image Processing, M.Tech in Embedded Systems from JNTUH; B.Tech in ECE from JNTUH. He has very good experience in Industry, teaching, Research & Development. He has 28 reputed International research Journals and 05 research conferences in his credit. He has guided 25 M.Tech Projects and 42 B.Tech Projects. He is peer reviewer for two International Journals. He organized various Technical Workshops, FDPs, Technical Seminars, Conferences in National and International. His research interest areas are Embedded Systems, Signal Processing, Image Processing Video Processing and Wireless Communications.

Authors Profile

Dr.R. Prakash Rao currently working as Associate Professor in the Department of ECE, Matrusri Engineering College affiliated to Osmania University, Hyderabad. He has completed Ph.D in VLSI from JNTUH, Hyderabad; M.Tech in Radar&Microwave from Andhra University; B.Tech in ECE from Ngarjuna University. He has 14 years of experience in teaching and 8 years of experience in Research & Development. He has 30 reputed International research Journals and 07 research conferences in his credit. His research interest areas are VLSI, VLSI with Signal Processing, Embedded Systems and Microwave Engineering.

Dr.S. Prabhakara Rao currently working as Professor in the Department of ECE, JBREC, affiliated to JNTUH, Hyderabad. He has completed PhD in ECE in the area of Wireless communication from JNTUH, Hyderabad; M.E in ECE with specialization of Communication Engineering from CBIT (Chaithanya Bharathi Institute of Technology) Hyderabad affiliated to Osmania University, Hyderabad; B.E in ECE from Vasavi College of Engineering, Hyderabad affiliated to Osmania University, Hyderabad. He has 22 years of experience in teaching and 10 years of experience in Research & Development. He has 13 reputed international research Journals and 12 research conferences in his credit. His research interest areas are wireless communications, wireless Networks, Networks security, Antenna Engineering. Embedded Systems and Microwave Engineering.

Gorre Narsimhulu currently working as Associate Professor in the Department of ECE, St. Peter's Engineering College affiliated to Jawaharlal Nehru Technological University (JNTUH), Hyderabad. He is pursuing Ph.D in wireless communications networks from JNTU Hyderabad, M.Tech in Digital systems and Computer electronics from College of Engineering JNTUH, B.Tech in ECE from JNTUH. He has very good experience in Industry, teaching, Research & Development. He worked as Professor for 5 years in Wolaitasodo University, SNNPR (ETHIOPIA). He has 11 reputed International research Journals and 04 research conferences in his credit. His research interest areas are wireless communications, Embedded Systems, CPLD & FPGA Networks and Image Processing and Digital System Design.

UNIT	CONTENTS	PAGE NO

UNIT 1

EMBEDDED SYSTEMS DESIGN

1.1. Introduction

This chapter introduces the reader to the world of embedded systems. Everything that we look around us today is electronic. The days are gone where almost everything was manual. Now even the food that we eat is cooked with the assistance of a microchip (oven) and the ease at which we wash our clothes is due to the washing machine. This world of electronic items is made up of embedded system.

In this chapter we will understand the basics of embedded system right from its definition.

An **embedded system** is a programmed controlled and operating system 'RTOS' with a dedicated function within a larger mechanical or electrical system, often with real-time computing constraints. It is *embedded* as part of a complete device often including hardware and mechanical parts. Embedded systems control many devices in common use today. Ninety-eight percent of all microprocessors are manufactured to serve as embedded system component.[4]

Examples of properties of typical embedded computers when compared with general-purpose counterparts are low power consumption, small size, rugged operating ranges, and low per-unit cost. This comes at the price of limited processing resources, which make them significantly more difficult to program and to interact with. However, by building intelligence mechanisms on top of the hardware, taking advantage of possible existing sensors and the existence of a network of embedded units, one can both optimally manage available resources at the unit and network levels as well as provide augmented functions, well beyond those available. For example, intelligent techniques can be designed to manage power consumption of embedded systems.

Modern embedded systems are often based on microcontrollers (i.e. CPUs with integrated memory or peripheral interfaces), but ordinary microprocessors (using external chips for memory and peripheral interface circuits) are also common, especially in more complex systems. In either case, the processor(s) used may be types ranging from general purpose to those specialized in certain class of computations or even custom designed for the application at hand. A common standard class of dedicated processors is the digital signal processor (DSP).

Since the embedded system is dedicated to specific tasks, design engineers can optimize it to reduce the size and cost of the product and increase the reliability and performance. Some embedded systems are mass-produced, benefiting from economies of scale.

Embedded systems range from portable devices such as digital watches and MP3 players, to large stationary installations like traffic lights, factory controllers, and largely complex systems like hybrid vehicles, MRI, and avionics. Complexity varies from low, with a single microcontroller chip, to very high with multiple units, peripherals and networks mounted inside a large chassis or enclosure.

An Embedded System on a Plug-in Card with Processor, Memory, Power Supply, and External Interfaces

Objectives

- To understand what is an Embedded System and then define it
- Look at embedded systems from a historical point of view
- Classify embedded systems
- Look at certain applications & purposes of embedded systems

History

One of the very first recognizably modern embedded systems was the Apollo Guidance Computer,[citation needed] developed ca. 1965 by Charles Stark Draper at the MIT Instrumentation Laboratory. At the project's inception, the Apollo guidance computer was considered the riskiest item in the Apollo project as it employed the then newly developed monolithic integrated circuits to reduce the size and weight. An early mass-produced embedded system was the Autonetics D-17 guidance computer for the Minuteman missile, released in 1961. When the Minuteman II went into production in 1966, the D-17 was replaced with a new computer that was the first high-volume use of integrated circuits.

Since these early applications in the 1960s, embedded systems have come down in price and there has been a dramatic rise in processing power and functionality. An early microprocessor for example, the Intel 4004 (released in 1971), was designed for calculators and other small systems but still required external memory and support chips. In 1978 National Engineering Manufacturers Association released a "standard" for programmable microcontrollers, including almost any computer-based controllers, such as single board computers, numerical, and event-based controllers.

As the cost of microprocessors and microcontrollers fell it became feasible to replace expensive knob-based analog components such as potentiometers and variable capacitors with up/down buttons or knobs read out by a microprocessor even in consumer products. By the early 1980s, memory, input and output system components had been integrated into the same chip as the processor forming a microcontroller. Microcontrollers find applications where a general-purpose computer would be too costly.

A comparatively low-cost microcontroller may be programmed to fulfill the same role as a large number of separate components. Although in this context an embedded system is usually more complex than a traditional solution, most of the complexity is contained within the microcontroller itself.

Very few additional components may be needed and most of the design effort is in the software. Software prototype and test can be quicker compared with the design and construction of a new circuit not using an embedded processor.

1.2. Definition of an Embedded System

An embedded system is a combination of 3 things:

A. Hardware

B. Software

C. Mechanical Components

And it is supposed to do one specific task only.

Example 1: Washing Machine

A washing machine from an embedded systems point of view has:

a. Hardware: Buttons, Display & buzzer, electronic circuitry.

b. b. Software: It has a chip on the circuit that holds the software which drives controls & monitors the various operations possible.

c. Mechanical Components: the internals of a washing machine which actually wash the clothes control the input and output of water, the chassis itself.

Example 2: Air Conditioner

An Air Conditioner from an embedded systems point of view has:

a. Hardware: Remote, Display & buzzer, Infrared Sensors, electronic circuitry.
b. Software: It has a chip on the circuit that holds the software which drives controls & monitors the various operations possible. The software monitors the external temperature through the sensors and then releases the coolant or suppresses it.
c. Mechanical Components: the internals of an air conditioner the motor, the chassis, the outlet, etc

An Embedded System is Designed to Do a Specific Job Only

Example: a washing machine can only wash clothes, an air conditioner can control the temperature in the room in which it is placed.

An embedded system will always have a chip (either microprocessor or microcontroller) that has the code or software which drives the system.

1.3. History of Embedded System

- The first recognised embedded system is the Apollo Guidance Computer (AGC) developed by MIT lab.
- AGC was designed on 4K words of ROM & 256 words of RAM.
- The clock frequency of first microchip used in AGC was 1.024 MHz.
- The computing unit of AGC consists of 11 instructions and 16 bit word logic.
- It used 5000 ICs.
- The UI of AGC is known DSKY (display/keyboard) which resembles a calculator type keypad with array of numerals.
- The first mass-produced embedded system was guidance computer for the Minuteman-I missile in 1961.
- In the year 1971 Intel introduced the world's first microprocessor chip called the 4004, was designed for use in business calculators. It was produced by the Japanese company Busicom.

1.4. Embedded System & General Purpose Computer

The Embedded System and the General purpose computer are at two extremes. The embedded system is designed to perform a specific task whereas as per definition the general purpose.

Computer is meant for general use. It can be used for playing games, watching movies, creating software, work on documents or spreadsheets etc.

Following are certain specific points of difference between embedded systems and general purpose computers:

Criteria	**General Purpose Computer**	**Embedded system**
Contents	It is combination of generic hardware and a general purpose OS for executing a variety of applications.	It is combination of special purpose hardware and embedded OS for executing specific set of applications
Operating System	It contains general purpose operating system	It may or may not contain operating system.
Alterations	Applications are alterable by the user.	Applications are non-alterable by the user.
Key factor .	Performance" is key factor.	Application specific requirements are key factors
Power Consumption	More	Less
Response Time	Not Critical	Critical for some applications

1.5. Classification of Embedded System

The classification of embedded system is based on following criteria's:

- On generation
- On complexity & performance
- On deterministic behavior
- On triggering

1.5.1. On Generation

1. First Generation (1G)

- Built around 8bit microprocessor & microcontroller.
- Simple in hardware circuit & firmware developed.
- Examples: Digital telephone keypads.

2. Second Generation (2G)

- Built around 16-bit μp & 8-bit μc.
- They are more complex & powerful than 1G μp & μc.
- Examples: SCADA systems

3. Third Generation (3G)

- Built around 32-bit μp & 16-bit μc.
- Concepts like Digital Signal Processors(DSPs).
- Application Specific Integrated Circuits (ASICs) evolved.
- Examples: Robotics, Media, etc.

4. Fourth Generation

- Built around 64-bit μp & 32-bit μc.
- The concept of System on Chips (SoC), Multicore Processors evolved.
- Highly complex & very powerful.
- Examples: Smart Phones.

1.5.2. On Complexity & Performance

1. Small-Scale

- Simple in application need.
- Performance not time-critical.
- Built around low performance & low cost 8 or 16 bitμp/μc.
- Example: an electronic toy

2. Medium-Scale

- Slightly complex in hardware & firmware requirement.
- Built around medium performance & low cost 16 or 32 bit μp/μc.
- Usually contain operating system.
- Examples: Industrial machines.

3. Large-Scale

- Highly complex hardware & firmware.
- Built around 32 or 64 bit RISC μp/μc or PLDs or Multicore Processors.
- Response is time-critical.
- Examples: Mission critical applications.

1.5.3. On Deterministic Behavior

- This classification is applicable for "Real Time" systems.
- The task execution behavior for an embedded system may be deterministic or non-deterministic.
- Based on execution behavior Real Time embedded systems are divided into Hard and Soft.

1.5.4. On Triggering

Embedded systems which are "Reactive" in nature can be based on triggering.

Reactive systems can be:

- Event triggered
- Time triggered

1.6. Application of Embedded System

The application areas and the products in the embedded domain are countless.

1. Consumer Electronics: Camcorders, Cameras.
2. Household appliances: Washing machine, Refrigerator.
3. Automotive industry: Anti-lock breaking system (ABS), engine control.
4. Home automation & security systems: Air conditioners, sprinklers, fire alarms.
5. Telecom: Cellular phones, telephone switches.
6. Computer peripherals: Printers, scanners.
7. Computer networking systems: Network routers and switches.
8. Healthcare: EEG, ECG machines.
9. Banking & Retail: Automatic teller machines, point of sales.
10. Card Readers: Barcode, smart card readers.
11. Embedded Computer Sub-Assembly for Accupoll Electronic Voting Machine[8]
12. Embedded systems are commonly found in consumer, industrial, automotive, medical, commercial and military applications.
13. Telecommunications systems employ numerous embedded systems from telephone switches for the network to cell phones at the end user. Computer networking uses dedicated routers and network bridges to route data.
14. Consumer electronics include MP3 players, mobile phones, video game consoles, digital cameras, GPS receivers, and printers. Household appliances, such as microwave ovens, washing machines and dishwashers, include embedded systems to provide

flexibility, efficiency and features. Advanced HVAC systems use networked thermostats to more accurately and efficiently control temperature that can change by time of day and season. Home automation uses wired- and wireless-networking that can be used to control lights, climate, security, audio/visual, surveillance, etc., all of which use embedded devices for sensing and controlling.

15. Transportation systems from flight to automobiles increasingly use embedded systems. New airplanes contain advanced avionics such as inertial guidance systems and GPS receivers that also have considerable safety requirements. Various electric motors — brushless DC motors, induction motors and DC motors — use electric/electronic motor controllers. Automobiles, electric vehicles, and vehicles increasingly use embedded systems to maximize efficiency and reduce pollution. Other automotive safety systems include anti-lock braking system (ABS), Electronic Stability Control (ESC/ESP), traction control (TCS) and automatic four-wheel drive.
16. Medical equipment uses embedded systems for vital signs monitoring, electronic stethoscopes for amplifying sounds, and various medical imaging (PET, SPECT, CT, and MRI) for non-invasive internal inspections. Embedded systems within medical equipment are often powered by industrial computers.[9]
17. Embedded systems are used in transportation, fire safety, safety and security, medical applications and life critical systems, as these systems can be isolated from hacking and thus, be more reliable, unless connected to wired or wireless networks via on-chip 3G cellular or other methods for IoT monitoring and control purposes.[citation needed] For fire safety, the systems can be designed to have greater ability to handle higher temperatures and continue to operate. In dealing with security, the embedded systems can be self-sufficient and be able to deal with cut electrical and communication systems.
18. A new class of miniature wireless devices called motes are networked wireless sensors. Wireless sensor networking, WSN, makes use of miniaturization made possible by advanced IC design to couple full wireless subsystems to sophisticated sensors, enabling people and companies to measure a myriad of things in the physical world and act on this information through IT monitoring and control systems. These motes are completely self-contained, and will typically run off a battery source for years before the batteries need to be changed or charged.
19. Embedded Wi-Fi modules provide a simple means of wirelessly enabling any device that communicates via a serial port.

1.7. Purpose of Embedded System

1. Data Collection/Storage/Representation

- Embedded system designed for the purpose of data collection performs acquisition of data from the external world.
- Data collection is usually done for storage, analysis, manipulation and transmission.
- Data can be analog or digital.
- Embedded systems with analog data capturing techniques collect data directly in the form of analog signal whereas embedded systems with digital data collection mechanism converts the analog signal to the digital signal using analog to digital converters.
- If the data is digital it can be directly captured by digital embedded system.
- A digital camera is a typical example of an embedded System with data collection/storage/representation of data.
- Images are captured and the captured image may be stored within the memory of the camera. The captured image can also be presented to the user through a graphic LCD unit.

2. Data Communication

- Embedded data communication systems are deployed in applications from complex satellite communication to simple home networking systems.
- The transmission of data is achieved either by a wire-line medium or by a wire-less medium.
- Data can either be transmitted by analog means or by digital means.
- Wireless modules-Bluetooth, Wi-Fi.
- Wire-line modules-USB, TCP/IP.
- Network hubs, routers, switches are examples of dedicated data transmission embedded systems.

3. Data Signal Processing

- Embedded systems with signal processing functionalities are employed in applications demanding signal processing like speech coding, audio video codec, transmission applications etc.
- A digital hearing aid is a typical example of an embedded system employing data processing.

- Digital hearing aid improves the hearing capacity of hearing impaired person.

4. Monitoring

- All embedded products coming under the medical domain are with monitoring functions.
- Electro cardiogram machine is intended to do the monitoring of the heartbeat of a patient but it cannot impose control over the heartbeat.
- Other examples with monitoring function are digital CRO, digital multi-meters, and logic analyzers.

5. Control

- A system with control functionality contains both sensors and actuators.
- Sensors are connected to the input port for capturing the changes in environmental variable and the actuators connected to the output port are controlled according to the changes in the input variable.
- Air conditioner system used to control the room temperature to a specified limit is a typical example for CONTROL purpose.

6. Application Specific User Interface

- Buttons, switches, keypad, lights, bells, display units etc are application specific user interfaces.
- Mobile phone is an example of application specific user interface.
- In mobile phone the user interface is provided through the keypad, system speaker, vibration alert etc.

1.8. Characteristics of an Embedded Systems

Embedded systems are designed to do some specific task, rather than be a general-purpose computer for multiple tasks. Some also have real-time performance constraints that must be met, for reasons such as safety and usability; others may have low or no performance requirements, allowing the system hardware to be simplified to reduce costs.

Embedded systems are not always standalone devices. Many embedded systems consist of small parts within a larger device that serves a more general purpose. For example, the Gibson Robot Guitar features an embedded system for tuning the strings, but the overall purpose of the Robot Guitar is, of course, to play music.[10] Similarly, an embedded system in an automobile provides a specific function as a subsystem of the car itself.

E-con Systems eSOM270 & eSOM300 Computer on Modules.

The program instructions written for embedded systems are referred to as firmware, and are stored in read-only memory or flash memorychips. They run with limited computer hardware resources: little memory, small or non-existent keyboard or screen.

User Interface

Embedded system text user interface using Micro VGA.

Embedded systems range from no user interface at all, in systems dedicated only to one task, to complex graphical user interfaces that resemble modern computer desktop operating systems. Simple embedded devices use buttons, LEDs, graphic or character LCDs (HD44780 LCD for example) with a simple menu system.

More sophisticated devices that use a graphical screen with touch sensing or screen-edge buttons provide flexibility while minimizing space used: the meaning of the buttons can change with the screen, and selection involves the natural behavior of pointing at what is desired. Handheld systems often have a screen with a "joystick button" for a pointing device.

Some systems provide user interface remotely with the help of a serial (e.g. RS-232, USB, I^2C, etc.) or network (e.g. Ethernet) connection. This approach gives several advantages: extends the capabilities of embedded system, avoids the cost of a display, simplifies BSP and allows one to build a rich user interface on the PC. A good example of this is the combination of an embedded web server running on an embedded device (such as an IP camera) or a network router. The user interface is displayed in a web browser on a PC connected to the device, therefore needing no software to be installed.

Processors in Embedded Systems

Embedded processors can be broken into two broad categories. Ordinary microprocessors (μP) use separate integrated circuits for memory and peripherals. Microcontrollers (μC) have on-chip peripherals, thus reducing power consumption, size and cost. In contrast to the personal computer market, many different basic CPU architectures are used since software is custom-developed for an application and is not a commodity product installed by the end user. Both Von Neumann as well as various degrees of Harvard architectures are used. RISC as well as non-RISC processors are found. Word lengths vary from 4-bit to 64-bits and beyond, although the most typical remain 8/16-bit. Most architectures come in a large number of different variants and shapes, many of which are also manufactured by several different companies.

Numerous microcontrollers have been developed for embedded systems use. General-purpose microprocessors are also used in embedded systems, but generally, require more support circuitry than microcontrollers.

Ready-Made Computer Boards

PC/104 and PC/104+ are examples of standards for *ready-made* computer boards intended for small, low-volume embedded and ruggedized systems, mostly x86-based. These are often physically small compared to a standard PC, although still quite large compared to most simple (8/16-bit) embedded systems. They often use DOS, Linux, NetBSD, or an embedded real-time operating system such as MicroC/OS-II, QNX or VxWorks. Sometimes these boards use non-x86 processors.

In certain applications, where small size or power efficiency are not primary concerns, the components used may be compatible with those used in general purpose x86 personal computers. Boards such as the VIA EPIA range help to bridge the gap by being PC-compatible but highly integrated, physically smaller or have other attributes making them attractive to embedded engineers. The advantage of this approach is that low-cost commodity components may be used along with the same software development tools used for general software development. Systems built in this way are still regarded as embedded since they are integrated into larger devices and fulfill a single role. Examples of devices that may adopt this approach are ATMs and arcade machines, which contain code specific to the application.

However, most ready-made embedded systems boards are not PC-centered and do not use the ISA or PCI buses.

When a system-on-a-chip processor is involved, there may be little benefit to having a standardized bus connecting discrete components, and the environment for both hardware and software tools may be very different.

One common design style uses a small system module, perhaps the size of a business card, holding high density BGA chips such as an ARM-based system-on-a-chip processor and peripherals, external flash memory for storage, and DRAM for runtime memory. The module vendor will usually provide boot software and make sure there is a selection of operating systems, usually including Linux and some real time choices. These modules can be manufactured in high volume, by organizations familiar with their specialized testing issues, and combined with much lower volume custom mainboards with application-specific external peripherals.

Implementation of embedded systems has advanced so that they can easily be implemented with already-made boards that are based on worldwide accepted platforms. These platforms include, but are not limited to, Arduino and Raspberry Pi.

ASIC and FPGA Solutions

A common array for very-high-volume embedded systems is the system on a chip (SoC) that contains a complete system consisting of multiple processors, multipliers, caches and interfaces on a single chip. SoCs can be implemented as an application-specific integrated circuit (ASIC) or using a field-programmable gate array (FPGA).

Peripherals

A close-up of the SMSC LAN91C110 (SMSC 91x) chip, an embedded Ethernet chip.

Embedded systems talk with the outside world via peripherals, such as:

- Serial Communication Interfaces (SCI): RS-232, RS-422, RS-485, etc.
- Synchronous Serial Communication Interface: I2C, SPI, SSC and ESSI (Enhanced Synchronous Serial Interface).
- Universal Serial Bus (USB).
- Multi Media Cards (SD cards, Compact Flash, etc.)
- Networks: Ethernet, LonWorks, etc.
- Fieldbuses: CAN-Bus, LIN-Bus, PROFIBUS, etc.
- Timers: PLL(s), Capture/Compare and Time Processing Units
- Discrete IO: aka General Purpose Input/Output (GPIO)
- Analog to Digital/Digital to Analog (ADC/DAC)
- Debugging: JTAG, ISP, ICSP, BDM Port, BITP, and DB9 ports.

Tools

As with other software, embedded system designers use compilers, assemblers, and debuggers to develop embedded system software. However, they may also use some more specific tools:

- In circuit debuggers or emulators (see next section).
- Utilities to add a checksum or CRC to a program, so the embedded system can check if the program is valid.
- For systems using digital signal processing, developers may use a math workbench to simulate the mathematics.

- System level modeling and simulation tools help designers to construct simulation models of a system with hardware components such as processors, memories, DMA, interfaces, buses and software behavior flow as a state diagram or flow diagram using configurable library blocks. Simulation is conducted to select right components by performing power vs. performance trade-off, reliability analysis and bottleneck analysis. Typical reports that helps designer to make architecture decisions includes application latency, device throughput, device utilization, power consumption of the full system as well as device-level power consumption.
- A model-based development tool creates and simulate graphical data flow and UML state chart diagrams of components like digital filters, motor controllers, communication protocol decoding and multi-rate tasks.
- Custom compilers and linkers may be used to optimize specialized hardware.
- An embedded system may have its own special language or design tool, or add enhancements to an existing language such as Forth or Basic.
- Another alternative is to add a real-time operating system or embedded operating system
- Modeling and code generating tools often based on state machines

Software tools can come from several sources:

- Software companies that specialize in the embedded market
- Ported from the GNU software development tools
- Sometimes, development tools for a personal computer can be used if the embedded processor is a close relative to a common PC processor

As the complexity of embedded systems grows, higher level tools and operating systems are migrating into machinery where it makes sense. For example, cellphones, personal digital assistants and other consumer computers often need significant software that is purchased or provided by a person other than the manufacturer of the electronics. In these systems, an open programming environment such as Linux, NetBSD, OSGi or Embedded Java is required so that the third-party software provider can sell to a large market.

Embedded systems are commonly found in consumer, cooking, industrial, automotive, medical applications. Some examples of embedded systems are MP3 players, mobile phones, video game consoles, digital cameras, DVD players, and GPS. Household appliances, such as microwave ovens, washing machines and dishwashers, include embedded systems to provide flexibility and efficiency.

1.9. Debugging

Embedded debugging may be performed at different levels, depending on the facilities available. The different metrics that characterize the different forms of embedded debugging are: does it slow down the main application, how close is the debugged system or application to the actual system or application, how expressive are the triggers that can be set for debugging (e.g., inspecting the memory when a particular program counter value is reached), and what can be inspected in the debugging process (such as, only memory, or memory and registers, etc.).

From simplest to most sophisticated they can be roughly grouped into the following areas:

- Interactive resident debugging, using the simple shell provided by the embedded operating system (e.g. Forth and Basic)
- External debugging using logging or serial port output to trace operation using either a monitor in flash or using a debug server like the Remedy Debugger that even works for heterogeneous multicore systems.
- An in-circuit debugger (ICD), a hardware device that connects to the microprocessor via a JTAG or Nexus interface.[11] This allows the operation of the microprocessor to be controlled externally, but is typically restricted to specific debugging capabilities in the processor.
- An in-circuit emulator (ICE) replaces the microprocessor with a simulated equivalent, providing full control over all aspects of the microprocessor.
- A complete emulator provides a simulation of all aspects of the hardware, allowing all of it to be controlled and modified, and allowing debugging on a normal PC. The downsides are expense and slow operation, in some cases up to 100 times slower than the final system.
- For SoC designs, the typical approach is to verify and debug the design on an FPGA prototype board. Tools such as Certus[12] are used to insert probes in the FPGA RTL that make signals available for observation. This is used to debug hardware, firmware and software interactions across multiple FPGA with capabilities similar to a logic analyzer.
- Software-only debuggers have the benefit that they do not need any hardware modification but have to carefully control what they record in order to conserve time and storage space.[13]

Unless restricted to external debugging, the programmer can typically load and run software through the tools, view the code running in the processor, and start or stop its operation. The view of the code may be as HLL source-code, assembly code or mixture of both.

Because an embedded system is often composed of a wide variety of elements, the debugging strategy may vary. For instance, debugging a software- (and microprocessor-) centric embedded system is different from debugging an embedded system where most of the processing is performed by peripherals (DSP, FPGA, and co-processor). An increasing number of embedded systems today use more than one single processor core. A common problem with multi-core development is the proper synchronization of software execution. In this case, the embedded system design may wish to check the data traffic on the busses between the processor cores, which requires very low-level debugging, at signal/bus level, with a logic analyzer, for instance.

Tracing

Real-time operating systems (RTOS) often supports tracing of operating system events. A graphical view is presented by a host PC tool, based on a recording of the system behavior. The trace recording can be performed in software, by the RTOS, or by special tracing hardware. RTOS tracing allows developers to understand timing and performance issues of the software system and gives a good understanding of the high-level system behaviors. Commercial tools like RTXC Quadros or IAR Systems exists.

Reliability

Embedded systems often reside in machines that are expected to run continuously for years without errors, and in some cases recover by themselves if an error occurs. Therefore, the software is usually developed and tested more carefully than that for personal computers, and unreliable mechanical moving parts such as disk drives, switches or buttons are avoided.

Specific reliability issues may include:

- The system cannot safely be shut down for repair, or it is too inaccessible to repair. Examples include space systems, undersea cables, navigational beacons, bore-hole systems, and automobiles.
- The system must be kept running for safety reasons. "Limp modes" are less tolerable. Often backups are selected by an operator. Examples include aircraft navigation, reactor control systems, safety-critical chemical factory controls, train signals.
- The system will lose large amounts of money when shut down: Telephone switches, factory controls, bridge and elevator controls, funds transfer and market making, automated sales and service.

A variety of techniques are used, sometimes in combination, to recover from errors—both software bugs such as memory leaks, and also soft errors in the hardware:

- Watchdog Timer that resets the computer unless the software periodically notifies the watchdog subsystems with redundant spares that can be switched over to software "limp modes" that provide partial function.
- Designing with a Trusted Computing Base (TCB) architecture[14] ensures a highly secure & reliable system environment.
- A hypervisor designed for embedded systems, is able to provide secure encapsulation for any subsystem component, so that a compromised software component cannot interfere with other subsystems, or privileged-level system software [15]. This encapsulation keeps faults from propagating from one subsystem to another, improving reliability. This may also allow a subsystem to be automatically shut down and restarted on fault detection.
- Immunity Aware Programming.

High vs.Low Volume

For high volume systems such as portable music players or mobile phones, minimizing cost is usually the primary design consideration. Engineers typically select hardware that is just "good enough" to implement the necessary functions.

For low-volume or prototype embedded systems, general purpose computers may be adapted by limiting the programs or by replacing the operating system with a real-time operating system.

1.10. Embedded Software Architecture

There are several different types of software architecture in common use.

Simple Control Loop

In this design, the software simply has a loop. The loop calls subroutines, each of which manages a part of the hardware or software. Hence it is called a simple control loop or control loop.

Interrupt-Controlled System

Some embedded systems are predominantly controlled by interrupts. This means that tasks performed by the system are triggered by different kinds of events; an interrupt could be generated, for example, by a timer in a predefined frequency, or by a serial port controller receiving a byte.

These kinds of systems are used if event handlers need low latency, and the event handlers are short and simple. Usually, these kinds of systems run a simple task in a main loop also, but this task is not very sensitive to unexpected delays.

Sometimes the interrupt handler will add longer tasks to a queue structure. Later, after the interrupt handler has finished, these tasks are executed by the main loop. This method brings the system close to a multitasking kernel with discrete processes.

Cooperative Multitasking

A no preemptive multitasking system is very similar to the simple control loop scheme, except that the loop is hidden in an API.[1] The programmer defines a series of tasks, and each task gets its own environment to "run" in. When a task is idle, it calls an idle routine, usually called "pause", "wait", "yield", "nop" (stands for *no operation*), etc.

The advantages and disadvantages are similar to that of the control loop, except that adding new software is easier, by simply writing a new task, or adding to the queue.

Preemptive Multitasking or Multi-Threading

In this type of system, a low-level piece of code switches between tasks or threads based on a timer (connected to an interrupt). This is the level at which the system is generally considered to have an "operating system" kernel. Depending on how much functionality is required, it introduces more or less of the complexities of managing multiple tasks running conceptually in parallel.

As any code can potentially damage the data of another task (except in larger systems using an MMU) programs must be carefully designed and tested, and access to shared data must be controlled by some synchronization strategy, such as message queues, semaphores or a non-blocking synchronization scheme.

Because of these complexities, it is common for organizations to use a real-time operating system (RTOS), allowing the application programmers to concentrate on device functionality rather than operating system services, at least for large systems; smaller systems often cannot afford the overhead associated with a *generic* real-time system, due to limitations regarding memory size, performance, or battery life. The choice that an RTOS is required brings in its own issues, however, as the selection must be done prior to starting to the application development process. This timing forces developers to choose the embedded operating system for their device based upon current requirements and so restricts future options to a large extent.[16] The restriction of future options becomes more of an issue as product life decreases.

Additionally the level of complexity is continuously growing as devices are required to manage variables such as serial, USB, TCP/IP, Bluetooth, Wireless LAN, trunk radio, multiple channels, data and voice, enhanced graphics, multiple states, multiple threads, numerous wait states and so on. These trends are leading to the uptake of embedded middleware in addition to a real-time operating system.

Micro Kernels and Exokernels

A microkernel is a logical step up from a real-time OS. The usual arrangement is that the operating system kernel allocates memory and switches the CPU to different threads of execution. User mode processes implement major functions such as file systems, network interfaces, etc.

In general, micro kernels succeed when the task switching and intertask communication is fast and fail when they are slow.

Exokernels communicate efficiently by normal subroutine calls. The hardware and all the software in the system are available to and extensible by application programmers.

Monolithic Kernels

In this case, a relatively large kernel with sophisticated capabilities is adapted to suit an embedded environment. This gives programmers an environment similar to a desktop operating system like Linux or Microsoft Windows, and is therefore very productive for development; on the downside, it requires considerably more hardware resources, is often more expensive, and, because of the complexity of these kernels, can be less predictable and reliable.

Common examples of embedded monolithic kernels are embedded Linux and Windows CE.

Despite the increased cost in hardware, this type of embedded system is increasing in popularity, especially on the more powerful embedded devices such as wireless routers and GPS navigation systems. Here are some of the reasons:

- Ports to common embedded chip sets are available.
- They permit re-use of publicly available code for device drivers, web servers, firewalls, and other code.
- Development systems can start out with broad feature-sets, and then the distribution can be configured to exclude unneeded functionality, and save the expense of the memory that it would consume.

- Many engineers believe that running application code in user mode is more reliable and easier to debug, thus making the development process easier and the code more portable.[*citation needed*]
- Features requiring faster response than can be guaranteed can often be placed in hardware.

Additional Software Components

In addition to the core operating system, many embedded systems have additional upper-layer software components. These components consist of networking protocol stacks like CAN, TCP/IP, FTP, HTTP, and HTTPS, and also included storage capabilities like FAT and flash memory management systems. If the embedded device has audio and video capabilities, then the appropriate drivers and codes will be present in the system. In the case of the monolithic kernels, many of these software layers are included. In the RTOS category, the availability of the additional software components depends upon the commercial offering.

UNIT 2

CORE THE OF AN EMBEDDED SYSTEM

2.1. Objectives

After reading this chapter you will be able to:

- Understand the differenttypes of core i.e processor.
- Understand difference between microprocessor &microcontroller.
- Understand the classification of processors based on Bus Architecture, Instruction set Architecture and Endianness.
- Have an overview of processors from most simple and cheap to most expensive and complex,powerful.
- Understand what are sensors and actuators,communication interfaces.

2.2. Introduction

The first two chapters attempted on explain what an embedded system is about and what the working parts are. This chapter attempts to go deeper and explain the core of embedded system along with other related topics.

2.3. Core of Embedded Systems

Embedded systems are domain and application specific and are built around a central core. The core of the embedded system falls into any of the following categories:

1. General purpose and Domain Specific Processors
    - Microprocessors
    - Microcontrollers
    - Digital Signal Processors
2. Application Specific Integrated Circuits. (ASIC)
3. Programmable logic devices(PLD's)
4. Commercial off-the-shelf components (COTs)

General Purpose and Domain Specific Processor

- Almost 80% of the embedded systems are processor/ controller based.
- The processor may be microprocessor or a microcontroller or digital signal processor, depending on the domain and application.

Microprocessors

- A microprocessor is a silicon chip representing a central processing unit.
- A microprocessor is a dependent unit and it requires the combination of other hardware like memory, timer unit, and *interrupt* controller, etc. for properfunctioning.
- Developers of microprocessors.
    - Intel – *Intel 4004* – November 1971(4-bit).
        - Intel – *Intel4040.*
        - Intel – *Intel 8008* – April1972.
        - Intel – *Intel 8080* – April1974(8-bit).
    - Motorola – *Motorola 6800.* o Intel – *Intel8085* – 1976. o Zilog - *Z80* – July1976.
- Architectures used for processor design are Harvard or Von- Neumann.

Harvard architecture	Von-Neumann architecture
• It has separate buses for instruction as well as data fetching. • Easier to pipeline, so high performance can be achieve. • Comparatively high cost. • Since data memory and program memory are stored physically in different locations, no chances exist for accidental corruption of program memory.	• It shares single common bus for instruction and data fetching. • Low performance as compared to Harvard architecture. • It is cheaper. • Accidental corruption of program memory may occur if data memory and program memory are stored physically in the same chip,

- RISC and CISC are the two common Instruction Set Architectures (ISA) available for processor design.

RISC	CISC
• Reduced Instruction Set Computing • It contains lesser number of instructions. • Instruction pipelining and increased execution speed. • Orthogonal instruction set(allows each instruction to operate on any register and use any addressingmode. • Operations are performed on registers only, only memory operations are load and store. • A larger number of registers are available. • Programmer needs to write more code to execute a task since instructions are simpler ones. • It is single, fixed length instruction.	• Complex Instruction Set Computing • It contains greater number of instructions. • Instruction pipelining feature does not exist. • Non-orthogonal set (all instructions are not allowed to operate on any register and use any addressingmode. • Operations are performed either on registers or memory depending on instruction. • The number of general purpose registers are very limited. • Instructions are like macros in C language. A programmer can achieve the desired functionality with a single instruction which in turn provides the effect of using more simpler single instruction in RISC. • It is variable length instruction.

• Less silicon usage and pin count.	• More silicon usage since more additional decoder logic is required to implement the complex instruction decoding.
• With Harvard Architecture	• Can be Harvard or Von- Neumann Architecture.

Endiannes

- Endianness specifies the order which the data is stored in the memory by processor operations in a multi byte system.
- Based on Endiannes processors can be of two types:
  1. Little Endian Processors
  2. Big Endian Processors
- Little-endian means lower order data byte is stored in memory at the lowest address and the higher order data byte at the highest address. For e.g, 4 byte long integer Byte3, Byte2, Byte1, Byte0 will be store in the memory as follows:

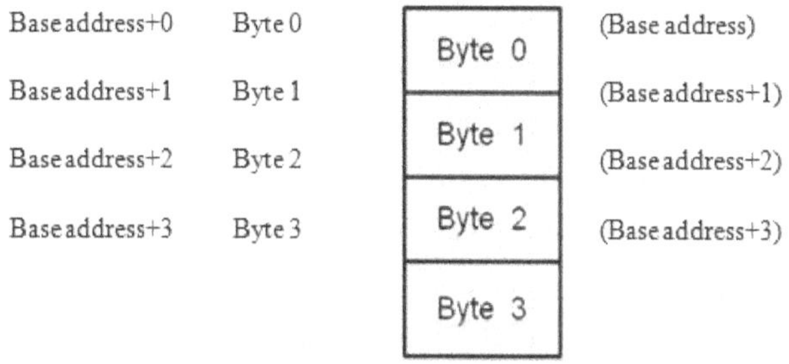

1. Big-endian means the higher order data byte is stored in memory at the lowest and the lower order data byte at the highest address. For e.g. a 4 byte integer Byte3, Byte2, Byte1, Byte0 will be stored in the memory as follows:

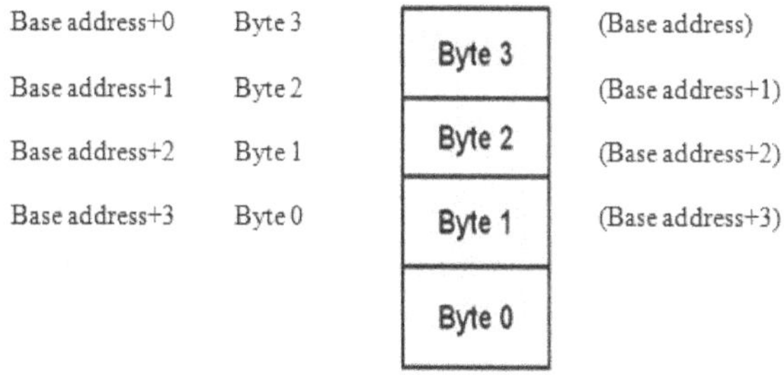

Microcontrollers

- A microcontroller is a highly integrated chip that contains a CPU, scratch pad RAM, special and general purpose register arrays, on chip ROM/FLASH memory for program storage, timer and interrupt control units and dedicated I/O ports.
- Texas Instrument's TMS 1000 Is considered as the world's first microcontroller.
- Some embedded system application require only 8 bit controllers whereas some requiring superior performance and computational needs demand 16/32 bit controllers.
- The instruction set of a microcontroller can be RISC or CISC.
- Microcontrollers are designed for either general purpose application requirement or domain specific application requirement.

Digital Signal Processors

- DSP are powerful special purpose 8/16/32 bit microprocessor designed to meet the computational demands and power constraints of today's embedded audio, video and communicationapplications.
- DSP are 2 to 3 times faster than general purpose microprocessors in signal processing applications. This is because of the architectural difference between DSP and general purpose microprocessors.
- DSPs implement algorithms inhardware which speeds up the execution whereas general purpose processor implement the algorithm in software and the speed of execution depends primarily on the clock for the processors.
- DSP includes following keyunits:

1. **Program memory:** It is a memory for storing the program required by DSP to process thedata.
2. **Data memory:** It is a working memory for storing temporary variables and data/signal to be processed.
3. **Computational engine:** It performs the signal processing in accordance with the stored program memory computational engine incorporated many specialized arithmetic units and each of them operates simultaneously to increase the execution speed. It also includes multiple hardware shifters for shifting operands and saves execution time.
4. **I/O unit:** It acts as an interface between the outside world and DSP. It is responsible for capturing signals to be processed and delivering the processed signals.

- Examples: Audio video signal processing, telecommunication and multimedia applications.
- SOP (Sum of Products) calculation, convolution, FFT (Fast Fourier Transform), DFT (Discrete Fourier Transform), etc are some of the operation performed by DSP.

Application Specific Integrated Circuits (ASIC)

- ASICs is a microchip design to perform a specific and unique applications.
- Because of using single chip for integrates several functions there by reduces the system development cost.
- Most of the ASICs are proprietary (which having some trade name) products, it is referred as Application Specific Standard Products (ASSP).
- As a single chip ASIC consumes a very small area in the total system. Thereby helps in the design of smaller system with high capabilities orfunctionalities.
- The developers of such chips may not be interested in revealing the internal detail of it.

Programmable Logic Devices (PLD's)

- A PLD is an electronic component. It used to build digital circuits which are reconfigurable.
- A logic gate has a fixed function but a PLD does not have a defined function at the time of manufacture.
- PLDs offer customers a wide range of logic capacity, features, speed, voltage characteristics.
- PLDs can be reconfigured to perform any number of functions at anytime.
- A variety of tools are available for the designers of PLDs which are inexpensive and help to develop, simulate and test the designs.
- PLDs having following two majortypes.

1. **CPLD (Complex Programmable Logic Device)**

CPLDs offer much smaller amount of logic up to 1000 gates.

2. **FPGAs (Field Programmable Gate Arrays)**

It offers highest amount of performance as well as highest logic density, the mostfeatures.

Advantages of PLDs

1. PLDs offer customer much more flexibility during the design cycle.
2. PLDs do not require long lead times for prototypes or production parts because PLDs are already on a distributors shelf and ready forshipment.
3. PLDs can be reprogrammed even after a piece of equipment is shipped to a customer

Commercial Off-the-Shelf Components (COTs)

1) A Commercial off the Shelf product is one which is used 'as- is'.
2) The COTS components itself may be develop around a general purpose or domain specific processor or an ASICs or a PLDs.
3) The major advantage of using COTS is that they are readily available in the market, are chip and a developer can cut down his/her development time to a greatextent
4) The major drawback of using COTS components in embedded design is that the manufacturer of the COTS component may withdraw the product or discontinue the production of the COTS at any time if rapid change in technology occurs.
5) Advantages of COTS:
   1. Ready to use
   2. Easy to integrate
   3. Reduces developmenttime
6) Disadvantages of COTS:
   1. No operational or manufacturing standard (all proprietary).
   2. Vendor or manufacturer may discontinue production of a particular COTSproduct.

2.4. Sensors & Actuators

Sensor

- A Sensor is used for takingInput
- It is a transducer that converts energy from one form to another for any measurement or control purpose
- Ex. A Temperature sensor

Actuator

- Actuator is used foroutput.
- It is a transducer that may be either mechanical or electrical which converts signals to corresponding physicalactions.

- Ex. LED (Light Emitting Diode)
- LED is a p-n junction diode and contains a **CATHODE** and **ANODE**
- For functioning the anode is connected to +ve end of power supply and cathode is connected to -ve end of power supply.
- The maximum current flowing through the LED is limited by connecting a RESISTOR in series between the power supply and LED as shown in the figure below

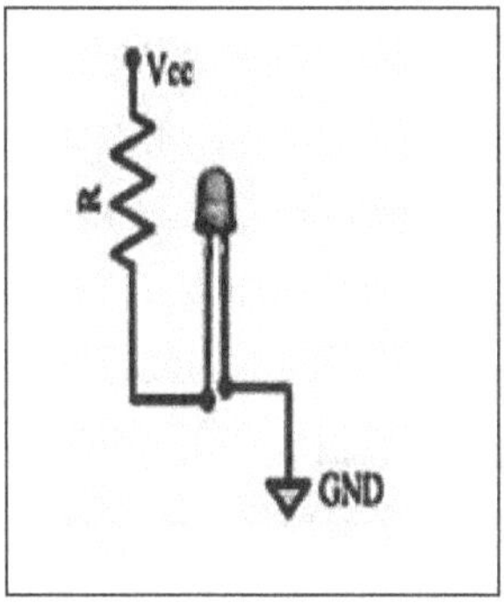

- There are two ways to microprocessor/microcontroller: interface an LED to a

1. **The Anode of LED is connected to the port pin and cathode to Ground :** In this approach the port pin sources the current to the LED when it is at logic high(ie. 1).
2. **The Cathode of LED is connected to the port pin and Anode to Vcc :** In this approach the port pin sources the current to the LED when it is at logic high (ie. 1). Here the port pin sinks the current and the LED is turned ON when the port pin is at Logic low (ie. 0)

2.5. Communication Interfaces

For any embedded system, the communication interfaces can broadly classified into:

1. Onboard Communication Interfaces

- These are used for internal communication of the embedded system i.e: communication between different components present on the system.
- Common examples of onboard interfacesare:
  - Inter Integrated Circuit (I2C)
  - Serial Peripheral Interface (SPI)
  - Universal Asynchronous Receiver Transmitter (UART)

- 1-Wire Interface
- Parallel Interface

- Example: Inter Integrated Circuit (I2C)
  - It is synchronous
  - Bi-directional, half duplex , two wire serial interface bus
  - Developed by Phillips semiconductors in 1980
  - It comprises of two buses:
    1. Serial clock –SCL
    2. Serial Data – SDA
  - SCL generates synchronization clockpulses
  - SDA transmits data serially acrossdevices
  - I2C is a shared bus system to which many devices can be connected
  - Devices connected by I2C can act as either master or slave
  - The master device is responsible for controlling communication by initiating/ terminating data transfer.
  - Devices acting as slave wait for commands from the master and respond to those commands.

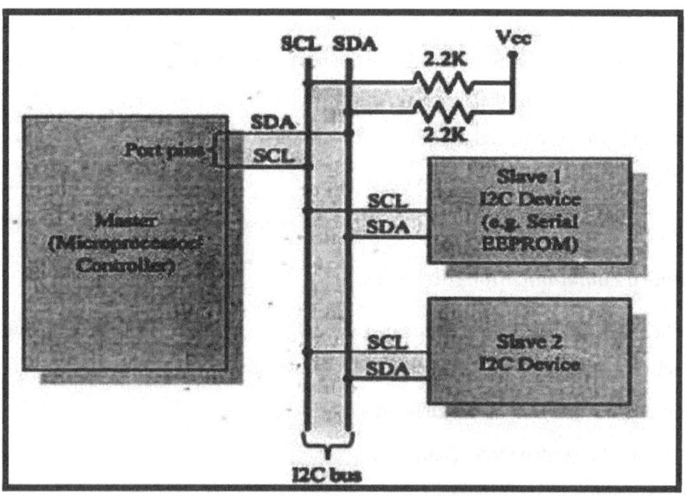

I2C Bus Interfacing

2. *External or Peripheral Communication Interfaces*

- These are embedded components peripheral components/devices.
- Common examples of external interfaces are:
    - RS-232 C & RS-485
    - Universal Serial Bus (USB)
    - IEEE 1394 (Firewire)
    - Infrared (IrDA)
    - Bluetooth
    - Wi-Fi
    - Zig Bee
    - General Packet Radio Service (GPRS)
    - **Example: RS-232 C & RS-485**
    - It is wired, asynchronous, serial, full duplex communication.
    - RS 232 interface was developed by EIA (Electronic Industries Associates) In early 1960s
    - RS 232 is the extension to UART for external communications.
    - RS-232 logic levels use:
    - +3 to +25 volts to signify a "Space" (Logic 0)and
    - -3 to -25 volts to signify a "Mark" (logic 1).
    - RS 232 supports two different types of connectors :
    - **DB 9 and DB 25** as shown in figurebelow

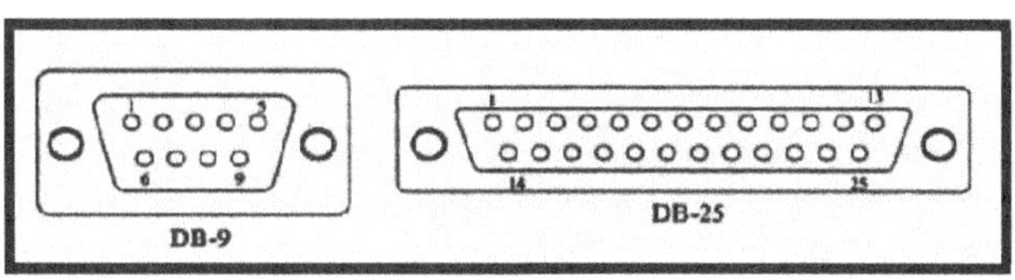

- RS 232 interface is a point to point communication interface and the devices involved are called as Data Terminating Equipment (DTE) And Data Communications Terminating Equipment (DCE)
- Embedded devices contain UART for serial transmission and generate signal levels as per TTL/CMOS logic.

- A level translator IC (like Max 232) is used for converting the signal lines from UART to RS 232 signal lines for communication.
- The vice versa is performed on the receivingside.
- Converter chips contain converters for both transmitters and receivers
- RS 232 is used only for point to point connections
- It is susceptible to noise and hence is limited to short distances only
- RS 422 is another serial interface fromEIA.
- It supports multipoint connections with 1 transmitter and 10 receivers.
- It supports data rates up to 100Kbps and distance up to 400 ft
- RS 485 is enhanced version of RS 422 and supports up to 32 transmitters and 32 receivers.

UNIT 3

EMBEDDED FIRMWARE

3.1. Introduction

Embedded firmware is the flash memory chip that stores specialized software running in a chip in an embedded device to control its functions.

Firmware in embedded systems fills the same purpose as a ROM but can be updated more easily for better adaptability to conditions or interconnecting with additional equipment.

Hardware makers use embedded firmware to control the functions of various hardware devices and systems much like a computer's operating system controls the function of software applications. Embedded firmware exists in everything from appliances so simple you might not imagine they had computer control, like toasters, to complex tracking systems in missiles. The toaster would likely never need updating but the tracking system sometimes does. As the complexity of a device increases, it often makes sense to use firmware in case of design errors that an update might correct.

Embedded firmware is used to control the limited, set functions of hardware devices and systems of greater complexity but still gives more appliance-like usage instead of a series of terminal commands. Embedded firmware functions are activated by external controls or external actions of the hardware. Embedded firmware and ROM-based embedded software often have communication links to other devices for functionality or to address the need for the device to be adjusted, calibrated or diagnosed or to output log files. It is also through these connections that someone might attempt embedded device hacking.

Embedded software varies in complexity as much the devices it is used to control. Although *embedded software* and *embedded* firmware are sometimes used synonymously, they are not exactly the same thing. For example, embedded software may run on ROM chips. Also, embedded software is often the only computer code running on a piece of hardware while firmware can also refer to the chip that houses a computer's EFI or BIOS, which hands over control to an OS that in turn launches and controls programs.

3.2. Reset Circuit or Power-on Reset (PoR)

A power-on reset (PoR) is a circuit that provides a predictable, regulated voltage to a microprocessor or microcontroller with the initial application of power. The PoR system ensures that the microprocessor or microcontroller will start in the same condition every time that it is powered up.

A PoR system can be a peripheral, but in sophisticated processors or controllers the PoR is integrated on the main chip. The most basic PoR system can comprise a resistor and capacitor connected together with values tailored so that, when power is first applied, the capacitor takes a predictable and constant time to charge up. For computer use, however, additional components are often required, including a circuit called a Schmitt trigger. When the PoR circuit is designed, the charge-up time should be adjusted by trial and error so that all of the processor or controller circuits can set themselves to the correct initial values before the computer begins to function.

A well-designed PoR circuit can ensure that when power is applied to a computer, it will start up properly every time (or almost every time), and will never (or rarely) freeze up right away. This feature not only saves the user a great deal of frustration, but it offers a last resort in case of a stubborn system crash: the so-called cold boot, where the computer is completely powered-down for a minute or two, and then powered-up all over again.

- The reset pin of a microcontroller is either active high or active low.
- Let us consider 8051 microcontroller.
- The reset pin of 8051 active high. Whenever power is switched on, positive going pulse should be present for 2 machine cycles on this pin.
- Reset Circuit for microcontroller 8051 is as follows:

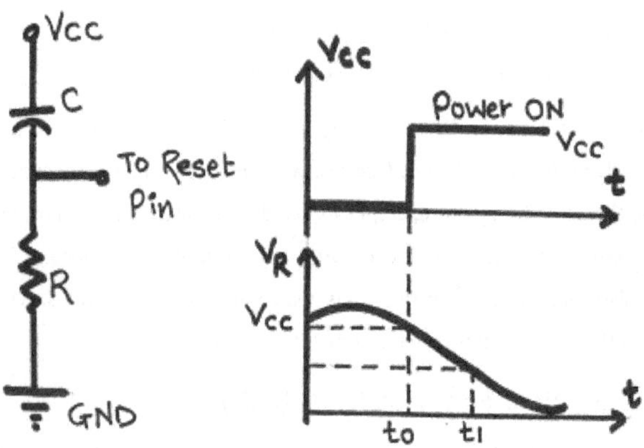

- At t0, the power supply is switched on, the supply voltage Vcc appears across the RC network. The entire voltage across resistor R, so VR is approximately equal to Vcc. This resets the 8051 microcontroller.
- Once the capacitor charges, then VR start decreasing and reach approximately 0V. This removes the reset signal. The (t1-t0) is reset time.

3.3. Brownout Reset Protection Circuit

A Brownout Near Tokyo Tower in Tokyo, Japan

A **brownout** is an intentional or unintentional drop in voltage in an electrical power supply system. Intentional brownouts are used for load reduction in an emergency.[1] The reduction lasts for minutes or hours, as opposed to short-term voltage sag (or dip). The term brownout comes from the dimming experienced by incandescent lighting when the voltage sags. A voltage reduction may be an effect of disruption of an electrical grid, or may occasionally be imposed in an effort to reduce load and prevent a power outage, known as a blackout.[2]

In some media reports the term *brownout* refers to an intentional or unintentional power outage or blackout of some areas rather than to a drop in voltage.

Different types of electrical apparatus will react in different ways to a sag. Some devices will be severely affected, while others may not be affected at all.

The heat output of any resistance device, such as an electric space heater, is equal to the true power consumption, which is an increasing function of the applied voltage. If the resistance stays constant, power consumption is proportional to the square of the applied voltage. Therefore, a significant reduction of heat output will occur with a relatively small reduction in voltage. An incandescent lamp will dim due to lower heat creation in the filament, as well as lower conversion of heat to light. Generally speaking, no damage will occur but functionality will be impaired.

Commutated electric motors, such as universal motors, will run at reduced speed or reduced torque. Depending on the motor design, no harm may occur. However, under load, the motor may draw more current due to the reduced back-EMF developed at the lower armature speed. Unless the motor has ample cooling capacity, it may eventually overheat and burn out.

An induction motor will draw more current to compensate for the decreased voltage, which may lead to overheating and burnout. If a substantial part of a grid's load is electric motors, reducing voltage may not actually reduce load and can result in damage to customers' equipment.

An unregulated direct current supply will produce a lower output voltage for electronic circuits. The output ripple voltage will decrease in line with the usually reduced load current. In a CRT television, the reduced output voltage can be seen as the screen image shrinking in size and becoming dim and fuzzy.

A linear direct current regulated supply will maintain the output voltage unless the brownout is severe and the input voltage drops below the drop out voltage for the regulator, at which point the output voltage will fall and high levels of ripple from the rectifier/reservoir capacitor will appear on the output.

A switched-mode power supply which has a regulated output will be affected. As the input voltage falls, the current draw will increase to maintain the same output voltage and current, until such a point that the power supply malfunctions.

Brownouts can cause unexpected behaviour in systems with digital control circuits. Reduced voltages can bring control signals below the threshold at which logic circuits can reliably detect which state is being represented. As the voltage returns to normal levels the logic can latch at an incorrect state; even can't happen states become possible. The seriousness of this effect and whether steps need to be taken by the designer to prevent it depends on the nature of the equipment being controlled; for instance, a brownout may cause a motor to begin running backwards.

Power Outage

A **power outage** (also called a **power cut**, a **power out**, a **power blackout**, **power failure** or a **blackout**) is a short-term or a long-term loss of the electric power to a particular area.

There are many causes of power failures in an electricity network. Examples of these causes include faults at power stations, damage to electric transmission lines, substations or other parts of the distribution system, a short circuit, or the overloading of electricity mains.

Power failures are particularly critical at sites where the environment and public safety are at risk. Institutions such as hospitals, sewage treatment plants, mines, shelters and the like will usually have backup power sources such as standby generators, which will automatically start up when electrical power is lost. Other critical systems, such as telecommunication, are also required to have emergency power. The battery room of a telephone exchange usually has arrays of lead-acid batteries for backup and also a socket for connecting a generator during extended periods of outage.

A brownout reset is a circuit that causes a computer processor to reset (or reboot) in the event of a brownout, which is a significant drop in the power supply output voltage.

Without a brownout reset circuit or an uninterruptible power supply (UPS) that maintains the full normal operating voltage for the processor when a brownout occurs, a processor can malfunction or lock up. In some cases, if a processor receives an abnormally low voltage and continues to operate anyway, it will produce nonsensical output.

Brownouts can occur for brief intervals or over extended periods. They commonly occur on utility lines at times of exceptional power demand, such as during heat waves or after natural disasters. In a computer, a brownout can also occur as a result of a problem with the internal power supply that converts the AC utility power to the DC used by a computer's internal electronic components.

3.4. Oscillator Unit

An oscillator is a mechanical or electronic device that works on the principles of oscillation: a periodic fluctuation between two things based on changes in energy. Computers, clocks, watches, radios, and metal detectors are among the many devices that use oscillators.

A clock pendulum is a simple type of mechanical oscillator. The most accurate timepiece in the world, the atomic clock, keeps time according to the oscillation within atoms. Electronic oscillators are used to generate signals in computers, wireless receivers and transmitters, and audio-frequency equipment, particularly music synthesizers. There are many types of electronic oscillators, but they all operate according to the same basic principle: an oscillator always employs a sensitive amplifier whose output is fed back to the input in phase. Thus, the signal regenerates and sustains itself. This is known as positive feedback. It is the same process that sometimes causes unwanted "howling" in public-address systems.

The frequency at which an oscillator works is usually determined by a quartz crystal. When a direct current is applied to such a crystal, it vibrates at a frequency that depends on its thickness, and on the manner in which it is cut from the original mineral rock. Some oscillators employ combinations of inductors, resistors, and/or capacitors to determine the frequency. However, the best stability (constancy of frequency) is obtained in oscillators that use quartz crystals.

In a computer, a specialized oscillator, called the clock, serves as a sort of pacemaker for the microprocessor. The clock frequency (or clock speed) is usually specified in megahertz (MHz), and is an important factor in determining the rate at which a computer can perform instructions.

3.5. Purpose of Unit Oscillator Section

Introduction

The Type 1218-A Unit Oscillator (Figm-e 1) is a general-purpose power source for the radio-frequency laboratory. Covering the frequency range from 900-2000 Me, it can be used to drive bridges, slotted lines, impedance comparators, admittance meters, and other measuring instruments. In combination with Type 874 Coaxial Elements and other basic instruments of the General Radio Unit Line, Unit Oscillators can, in many applications, replace more expensive equipment that is not always available. 1.1.2 With a Type 874 Voltmeter and Attenuator, known output voltages can be provided for receiver testing. Connected to a Type 874 Mixer, the Unit Oscillator can provide the local signal in a heterodyne receiver system to convert the Type 1216-A Unit 1-F Amplifier or any low-frequency communications receiver into a detector for uhf signals. 1.1.3 Provisions have been made to apply external modulating voltages for various modes of operation, including square-wave, sine-wave, and pulse modulation, and automatic output control. 1.1.4 With the Type 1000-P7 Balanced Modulator, linear 100-percent amplitude modulation is possible over a modulating frequency range of 0 to 20 Me. The same modulator can be used for pulsing where it provides high carrier suppression and fast rise-time characteristics, unaffected by the relatively long build-up time of the oscillator. Automatic output control is of great advantage when frequency characteristics are obtained by manual methods, and is almost indispensable for a swept oscillator. The output of the Type 1218-A Unit Of scillator can be monitored by a voltmeter and can be kept constant by the Type 1263-B Amplitude-Regulating Power Supply.

Real Time Clock

Dallas Semiconductor (DS1387) Real-Time Clock from an Older PC. This Version also Contains a Battery-Backed SRAM

A **real-time clock** (**RTC**) is a computer clock (most often in the form of an integrated circuit) that keeps track of the current time.

Although the term often refers to the devices in personal computers, servers and embedded systems, RTCs are present in almost any electronic device which needs to keep accurate time. A common RTC used in single-board computers is the Maxim Integrated DS1307.

The term *real-time clock* is used to avoid confusion with ordinary hardware clocks which are only signals that govern digital electronics, and do not count time in human units. RTC should not be confused with real-time computing, which shares its three-letter acronym but does not directly relate to time of day.

Purpose

Although keeping time can be done without an RTC,[1] using one has benefits:

- Low power consumption[2] (important when running from alternate power).
- Frees the main system for time-critical tasks.
- Sometimes more accurate than other methods.

A GPS receiver can shorten its startup time by comparing the current time, according to its RTC, with the time at which it last had a valid signal.[3] If it has been less than a few hours, then the previous ephemeris is still usable.

Timing

Most RTCs use a crystal oscillator,[7][8] but some have the option of using the power line frequency.[9] In many cases, the oscillator's frequency is 32.768 kHz.[7] This is the same frequency used in quartz clocks and watches, and for the same reasons, namely that the frequency is exactly 2^{15} cycles per second, is a convenient rate to use with simple binary counter circuits.

Many commercial RTC ICs are accurate to less than 5 parts per million.[10] In practical terms, this is good enough to perform celestial navigation, the classic task of a chronometer. In 2011, Chip-scale atomic clocks were invented. Although more expensive, they keep time within 100 nanoseconds

This Chip, Labeled ODIN, is a Generic Equivalent to a Particular Dallas RTC

Many integrated circuit manufacturers make RTCs, including Epson, Intersil, IDT, Maxim, NXP Semiconductors, Texas Instruments, STMicroelectronics and Ricoh.

The RTC was introduced to PC compatibles by the IBM PC/AT in 1984, which used a Motorola MC146818 RTC. Later, Semiconductor made compatible RTCs, which were often used in older personal computers, and are easily found on motherboards because of their distinctive black battery cap and silkscreened logo.

In newer systems, the RTC is integrated into the southbridge chip.[12]

Some microcontrollers have a real-time clock built in, generally only the ones with many other features and peripherals.

Radio-based RTCs

Some modern computers receive clock information by digital radio and use it to promote time-standards. There are two common methods: Most cell phone protocols (e.g. LTE) directly provide the current local time. If an internet radio is available, a computer may use the network time protocol. Computers used as local time servers occasionally use GPS[13] or ultra-low frequency radio transmissions broadcast by a national standards organization (i.e. a radio clock[14]).

Historic RTCs

Some older computer designs such as Novas and PDP-8s[15] used a real-time clock that was notable for its high accuracy, simplicity, flexibility and low cost. The computer's power supply produces a pulse at logic voltages for either each half-wave or each zero crossing of AC mains. A wire carries the pulse to an interrupt. The interrupt handler software counts cycles, seconds, etc. In this way, it can provide an entire clock and calendar.

The clock also usually formed the basis of computers' software timing chains; e.g. it was usually the timer used to switch tasks in an operating system. Counting timers used in modern computers provide similar features at lower precision, and may trace their requirements to this type of clock. (e.g. in the PDP-8, the mains-based clock, model DK8EA, came first, and was later followed by a crystal-based clock, DK8EC.)

A software-based clock must be set each time its computer is turned on. Originally this was done by computer operators. When the Internet became commonplace, network time protocols were used to automatically set clocks of this type.

In Europe, North America and some other grids, this RTC works because the frequency of the AC mains is adjusted to have a long-term frequency accuracy as good as the national standard clocks. That is, in those grids this RTC is superior to quartz clocks and less costly.

This design of RTC is not practical in portable computers or grids (e.g. in South Asia) that do not regulate the frequency of AC mains. Also it might be thought inconvenient without Internet access to set the clock.

3.6. Embedded Firmware Design Approaches and Development Languages Introduction

Every digital device that is driven by a CPU core processes some sort of digital information. Not all of them are digital data. In fact, major portion of them are some kind of instruction to the CPU. As we all know, they are patterns of zeros and ones. In groups, those zeros and ones are called as nibbles (a group of 4), bytes (A group of 8), half word (group of 16) and word (group of 32). Every microcontroller comes with an inbuilt memory. They store instruction and data. When their CPU runs, they fetch the code from the memory. They obtain data either from memory or from external I/O.

The collection of the data and the code together is called **firmware.** And the algorithm that the programmer follows is called a **program.** The final output of a program is a binary bit stream that is executed by the CPU. We also call them as hex code.

If someone writes an error free program and generates hex code by himself/herself, no doubt it will run. But its laborious, time consuming and prone to error. So as humans always do, less laborious and less problematic solution of this particular problem has been found out! Computer languages are brought to work for code generation.

The basic target of any compiler is to generate hex code. Whether it is an executable file or the collection of the hexadecimal code stored in a file called "HEX File". For embedded system, it always comes out in form of HEX files that is executed by the CPU (Note that few processors like ARM supports direct JAVA byte code execution). It is later downloaded into target microcontrollers (we call this process as "***burning program to microcontroller***").

Embedded C

C is the immediate advance language to assembly language for software development. Though microcontrollers provided limited processing power, embedded C developers managed to integrate most popular functions of ANSI C to embedded C. As discussed previously, sometimes the IDE developers provide some extensions. They use keywords, various macros and functions to facilitate programming for microcontrollers.

Each manufacturers may publish multiple architectures. And each architecture must have at least one compiler to support programming. Their architectural difference stops to use one single compiler for all families. Few specific difference may demand a huge programming in the compilers framework. So usually manufacturers avoid publishing a micro controller with very different architecture. The compilers of manufacturers' usually doesn't support other IC manufacturers' microcontrollers. The major reason is that it is very difficult to develop a single standard IDE due to large variety of microcontroller family. Here is a list of few IDE published by popular manufacturers.

Publisher	IDE
Renesas	Cube Suite Plus
Texas Instruments	IAR Workbench
National Instruments	Lab VIEW
NXP (a Phillips undertaken company)	LPC Xpresso
Microchip	MPLab SIM
Atmel	AVR Studio
ARM	Keil Microvision

Java

Most of the embedded IDE doesn't support java programming. Yet, many JAVA application runs successfully in many devices. Recently, few IDEs are adopting JAVA for hex code generation. But this is not the major key to the success of JAVA in the field of embedded systems. Instead of adapting JAVA as a program development language, ARM adapted a technique to allow JAVA Byte code to be executed by a single microcontroller. JAVA byte code is the usual output of a java program. This allowed software professionals to develop JAVA based software and operating system to run on ARM powered devices. This allowed to use the existing talents in the IT sectors. This, in turn, pumped up production of gadgets running with JAVA based systems. Almost 90% of the mobile and portable devices comes with firmware developed with JAVA.

The impact of adapting JAVA by a microcontroller is a milestone. But efforts are there to make HEX code generation possible wit JAVA. The pioneer of this effort is Microchip Corporation. Their IDE MP Lab Sim supports embedded JAVA to develop a program. Nevertheless, they have to generate hex code for their microcontrollers.

3.7. Real Time OS based on Embedded Systems Design

1. What is Embedded Systems? Embedded systems also contain some type of inputs and outputs Inputs to the system generally take the form of sensors and probes, communication signals, or control knobs and buttons. Outputs are generally displays, communication signals, or changes to the physical world. E.g. microwave oven Real-

time embedded systems is one major subclass of embedded systems and time is most important part for this type of system

2. Example and History Air conditioner, Home security system, ATM machine all this are example of embedded system airplane's flight control system, This example are real time embedded in real time embedded system time is major factor In the earliest years of computers in 1930 –40s, computers were sometimes dedicated to a single purpose task. One of the first recognizably modern embedded system was the Apollo Guidance Computer, developed by Charles Stark Draper at the MIT Instrumentation Laboratory.
3. Real-time programming programming the processes or instruction set with constraints of time for its response, process with latencies, and process with deadlines. Procedure-oriented C and object-oriented programming C++ and Java languages are used in most embedded systems programming. Embedded programming is such that methods to optimize the system memory requirements are also used. For some embedded system which has more no. of hardware and memory management this type use RTOS for programming
4. Real-Time Operating System An RTOS is an OS for response time-controlled and event-controlled processes. It is very essential for large scale embedded systems. RTOS occupy little space from 10 KB to 100KB The main task of a RTOS is to manage there sources of the computer such that a particular operation executes in precisely the same amount of time every time it occur. Renesas automotive dashboard platform.
5. When RTOS is not necessary? Software for a large number of small-scale embedded system use no RTOS and these functions are incorporate d into the application software. For small-scaled systems, RTOS's function can be replaced by C. For example, instead of the memory allocation and de-allocation functions of RTOS, the C function , melloc and free can be used. Software can directly handle inter-process communication
6. When RTOS is necessary? However, RTOS is essential when... A common and effective way of handling of the hardware source calls from the interrupts I/O management with devices, files, mailboxes becomes simple using an RTOS Effectively scheduling and running and blocking of the tasks in cases of many tasks and many more..... In conclusion, an RTOS may not be necessary in a small-scaled embedded system. An RTOS is necessary when scheduling of multiple processes and devices is important.
7. Hard and Soft Real Time Systems Hard Real time system: Failure to meet such a dead line is considered to be a fatal fault and will lead to disastrous on sequences e.g. Response of the break system of a speeding Train approaching a Red Signal to the stop

command must come before the train crosses the Red signal. Soft Real time system : Failure to miss a Soft Deadline is undesirable but a few misses does no serious harm like occasional delay in an on line trading of stocks. However the system's overall performance becomes poorer and poorer as more and more jobs starts missing the deadline.

8. CPU Architectures & Structure of a RTOS 8051, ARM7,ARM9, IntelXscale, AVR, Blackfin, C167, Coldfire,, MIPS, MSP430, PIC, PowerPC, R8C, SHARC, ST6, SuperH, TLCS-47, TLCS-870, TLCS-900, Tricore, etc. The most important component of RTOS is its kernel (Monolithic & Microkernel). BSP or Board Support Package makes an RTOS target-specific (It's a processor specific code onto (processor) which we like to have our RTOS running).
9. Monolithic kernel Vs Microkernel Monolithic Kernel Microkernel RTOS Kernel Functions1. Task Management2. Inter task Communication & Synchronization3. Dynamic Memory Allocation4. Timers5. Devices I/O Supervisor
10. Task Management Set of services used to allow application software developers to design their software as a number of separate chunks of software each handling a distinct topic, a distinct goal, and sometimes its own real-time deadline. Main service offered is Task Scheduling controls the execution of application software tasks v can make them run in a very timely and responsive fashion.
11. Task Scheduling block diagram Task cancel Desired resources available.
12. Task Scheduling Non Real -time systems usually use Non-preemptive Scheduling. Once a task starts executing, it completes its full execution Most RTOS perform priority-based preemptive task scheduling. Basic rules for priority based preemptive task scheduling. The Highest Priority Task that is Ready to Run, will be the Task that Must be Running.
13. Priority based Preemptive Task Scheduling Every Task in a software application is assigned a priority. Higher Priority = Higher Need for Quick Response. Follows nested preemption
14. Nested Preemption Timeline for Priority-based Preemptive Scheduling
15. Task Switch (1) Each time the priority-based preemptive scheduler is alerted by an External world trigger / Software trigger it shall go through the following steps that constitute a Task Switch: Determine whether the currently running task should continue to run. Determine which task should run next. v Save the environment of the

task that was stopped (so it can continue later). Set up the running environment of the task that will run next. Allow the selected task to run.

16. Task Switch (2) A Non Real time operating system might do task switching only at timer tick times. Even with preemptive schedulers a large array of tasks is searched before a task switch. A Real time OS shall use Incrementally arranged tables to save on time.
17. Intertask Communication &Synchronization These services makes it possible to pass information from one task to another without information ever being damaged. Makes it possible for tasks to coordinate & productively cooperate with each other.
18. Inter-Task communication &Synchronization The most important communication b/w tasks in an OS is the passing of data from one task to another. Message Message Producer Task Receiver Task If messages are sent more quickly than they can be handled, the OS provides message queues for holding the messages until they can be processed.
19. Message passing in RTOS In RTOS, the OS copies a pointer to the message, delivers the pointer to the message-receiver task, and then deletes the copy of the pointer with message-sender task. Message Sender RAM Task Message Message Receiver RTOS Task msg_ptr msg_ptr
20. Dynamic Memory Allocation in RTOS RTOS does it by a mechanism known as Pools. Pools memory allocation mechanism allows application software to allocate chunks of memory of 4 to 8 different buffer sizes per pool. Pools avoid external memory fragmentation, by not permitting a buffer that is returned to the pool to be broken into smaller buffers in the future. When a buffer is returned the pool, it is put onto a free buffer list of buffers of its own size that are available for future re-use at their original buffer size
21. Device i/o and Time Management An RTOS kernel is often equipped with a device I/O management service to provide a uniform framework and supervision facility for an embedded system to organize and access large numbers of diverse hardware device drivers. In embedded systems, system and user tasks are often scheduled to perform after a specified duration. To provide such scheduling, there is a need for a periodical interrupt to keep track of time delays and timeout. Most RTOSs today offer both "relative timers" that work in units of ticks, and "absolute timers" that work with calendar date and time. For each kind of timer, RTOSs provide a "task delay" service, and also a "task alert" service based on the signaling mechanism (e.g. event flags).

Another timer service provided is in meeting task deadline by cooperating with task schedulers to determine whether tasks have met or missed their real-time deadlines.

22. Peripheral devices and protocols • Interfacing Serial/parallel ports, USB, I2C, PCMCIA, IDE • Communication Serial, Ethernet, Low bandwidth radio, IrDA, 802.11b based devices • User Interface LCD, Keyboard, Touch sensors, Sound, Digital pads, Webcams • Sensors A variety of sensors using fire, temperature, pressure, water level, seismic, sound, vision
23. Example of Rtos •Wind River Systems Linux based VxWorks •Embedded Debian Project pSOS convert Debian to an •QNX Software Systems embedded OS QNX •ETLinux •Mentor Graphics for PC104 SBC's VRTX •uCLinux •Palm Computing for microprocessors that don't PalmOS have MM •Mobile OS •uLinux (muLinux) SymbianOS distro fits on a single floppy

The Role of an RTOS in an Embedded System

An embedded system is a special computer system that is designed to perform dedicated functions with real-time computing constraints. It contains software, memory, and a processor that may be 8051micro-controller memory ROM or Pentium-IV processor memory RAM. It also contains different types of inputs and outputs. Inputs are in the form of probes and sensors, buttons, control knobs and communication signals. Outputs are changes made to the physical world, communication signals, and displays.

A real-time embedded system is the main subcategory of embedded systems that focuses on timely task execution. For instance, smart home security systems, ATM machines, and air conditioners are embedded systems and an airplane's flight control system is a real-time embedded system where time is a core factor.

A real-time operating system(RTOS) is software that supplements computer hardware complexities. Almost all real-time operating systems provide threading, the illusion that processors can execute many tasks at the same time. System software that offers primitive I/O and a little more than threading is referred to as a tiny kernel. Widely used commercial tiny kernels include wind kernel and Nucleus. Operating systems operate applications in processes whereby the operating system monitors errors in processes, prevents the processes from destroying anything but themselves, and later recovers smoothly once the process terminates unexpectedly. Commonly used real-time operating systems include QNX, LynxOS, and OS-9.

Real-time software is ideal for deadline-specific systems. It ensures that prediction of tasks' execution durations is done accurately. However, the margin of error varies from 200 μs to 2 μs based on the hardware in use. RTOSs are highly responsive and fast. Operating systems support processes that give programs the illusion that they are running on their own machine. For embedded systems, a process is a thread with protection that recovers resources once a process terminates unintentionally to prevent resource leaks. The OS relies on software techniques, hardware memory protection and supervisor/user distinction within the processor instruction set to prevent process accidents or malicious actions from damaging other processes and the operating system. This action isolates problems affecting the processes, eases debugging and makes fault recovery easier, leading to a more robust system.

Programmers or system users accustomed to operating systems such as Windows and Linux appreciate other aspects of an embedded RTOS. For instance; real-time operating systems are designed to run indefinitely and flawlessly without requiring a reboot. They are designed for use in systems that have less memory as compared to normal operating systems; less than 100 Kbytes may not be enough but less than a megabyte works fine. An RTOS tends to perform better on tasks that must be executed within a short time. They may, however, be slow at big tasks as compared to regular operating systems because RTOSs are designed to respond to events promptly and run effectively under heavy loads.

Real-time operating systems are the only practical solution for use in embedded systems, especially in scenarios were multiple control loops are required to behave predictably under controlled priority levels.

3.8. What Are Real-Time Embedded Systems?

Real-time systems are computer systems that monitor, respond to, or control an external environment. This environment is connected to the computer system through sensors, actuators, and other input-output interfaces. It may consist of physical or biological objects of any form and structure. Often humans are part of the connected external world, but a wide range of other natural and artificial objects, as well as animals, are also possible.

The computer system must meet various timing and other constraints that are imposed on it by the real-time behavior of the external world to which it is interfaced. Hence comes the name *real time.* Another name for many of these systems is *reactive systems,* because their primary purpose is to respond to or react to signals from their environment. A real-time computer system may be a component of a larger system in which it is embedded; reasonably, such a computer component is called an *embedded system.*

Applications and examples of real-time systems are ubiquitous and proliferating, appearing as part of our commercial, government, military, medical, educational, and cultural infrastructures. Included are

- Vehicle systems for automobiles, subways, aircraft, railways, and ships.
- Traffic control for highways, airspace, railway tracks, and shipping lanes.
- Process control for power plants, chemical plants, and consumer products such as soft drinks and beer.
- Medical systems for radiation therapy, patient monitoring, and defibrillation.
- Military uses such as firing weapons, tracking, and command and control.
- Manufacturing systems with robots.
- Telephone, radio, and satellite communications.
- Computer games.
- Multimedia systems that provide text, graphic, audio, and video interfaces.
- Household systems for monitoring and controlling appliances.
- Building managers that control such entities as heat, lights, doors, and elevators.

3.9. Embedded System and Its Real Time Applications

October 12, 2017 by Ravi Leave a Comment

An article on Embedded System and its Real Time Applications. Focuses on different topics like What is an Embedded System, What are the Real Time Applications of Embedded Systems, What is the Future of Embedded Systems, etc.

The World is filled with Embedded Systems. The development of Microcontroller has paved path for several Embedded System application and they play a significant role (and will continue to play in the future as well) in our modern day life in one way or the other.

Starting from consumer electronics like Digital Cameras, DVD Players to high end and advanced systems like Flight Controllers and Missile Guidance Systems, embedded systems are omnipresent and became an important part of our life.

The way we live our life has been significantly improved with the utilization of Embedded Systems and they will continue to be an integral part of our lives even tomorrow.

Another important concept we are hearing these days is Real – Time Systems. In a real time system, Real Time Computing takes place, where a computer (an Embedded System) must generate response to events within certain time limits.

Before going in to the details of Real Time Applications of Embedded Systems, we will first see what an Embedded System is, what is a real time system and what is real time operating system.

3.10. What is an Embedded System?

An Embedded System is a combination of Hardware and Software. My desktop computer also has hardware and software. Does that mean a desktop computer is also an Embedded System? NO. A desktop computer is considered a general purpose system as it can do many different tasks that too simultaneously. Some common tasks are playing videos, working on office suites, editing images (or videos), browsing the web, etc.

An Embedded System is more of an application oriented system i.e. it is dedicated to perform a single task (or a limited number of tasks, but all working for a single main aim).

An example for embedded system, which we use daily, is a Wireless Router. In order to get wireless internet connectivity on our mobile phones and laptops, we often use routers. The task of a wireless router is to take the signal from a cable and transmit it wirelessly. And take wireless data from the device (like a mobile) and send it through the cable.

Even though the task seems simple, there are many individual sub tasks involved in this process. Some of these tasks include assigning Dynamic IP Addresses to clients (devices), managing data from each device, security and encryption, transmit and receive data, etc.

Components of Embedded System

An Embedded System consists of four main components. They are the Processor (Microprocessor or Microcontroller), Memory (RAM and ROM), Peripherals (Input and Output) and Software (main program).

Processor: The heart of an Embedded System is the Processor. Based on the functionality of the system, the processor can be anything like a General Purpose Processor, a single purpose processor, an Application Specific Processor, a microcontroller or an FPGA.

Memory: Memory is another important part of an embedded system. It is divided in to RAM and ROM. Memory in an Embedded System (ROM to be specific) stores the main program and RAM stores the program variables and temporary data.

Peripherals: In order to communicate with the outside world or control the external devices, an Embedded System must have Input and Output Peripherals. Some of these peripherals include Input / Output Ports, Communication Interfaces, Timers and Counters, etc.

Software: All the hardware work according to the software (main program) written. Software part of an Embedded System includes initialization of the system, controlling inputs and outputs, error handling etc.

NOTE: Many Embedded Systems, usually small to medium scaled systems, generally consists of a Microcontroller as the main processor. With the help of a Microcontroller, the processor, memory and few peripherals will be integrated in to a single device.

3.11. What is a Real Time Embedded System?

A subcategory of Embedded Systems is the Real Time Embedded Systems. A Real Time Embedded System is a type of computer system with timing constraints i.e. a system which responds to external events or input stimuli in a timely fashion (within finite and specified time).

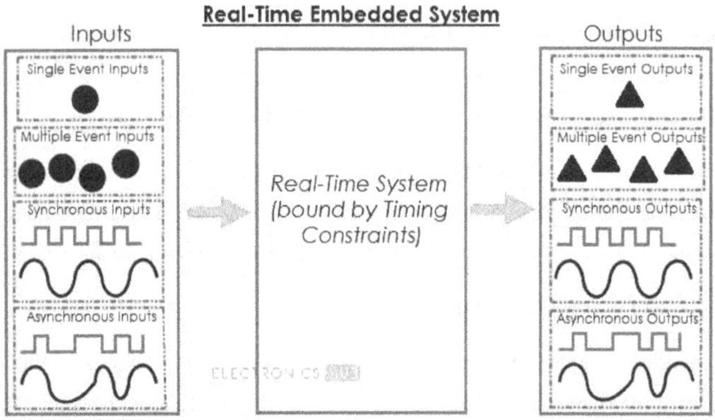

Here, Timing Constrains include Response Time, Start Time and Finish Time i.e. time taken to respond to the event, time at which the response to the even starts and time at which the response is given. Let us take a real world example of a Real Time System.

Consider a Weapons Defense System, whose job is to shoot down incoming missiles and protect the Naval Destroyer. This Weapons Defense System consists of three sub-systems: a Radar System, a Control System and a Weapons Firing System.

The Control System acts as a Command and Decision System, which is a controlling system and the Radar System and Weapons Firing System are the controlled systems. Now we will see how this Real Time System works in a real world scenario.

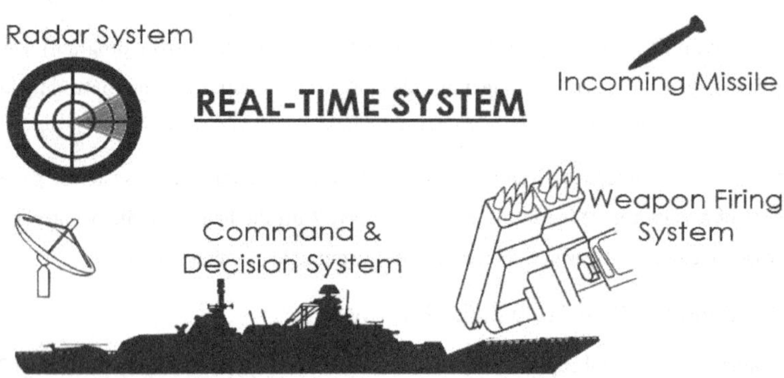

First, the Radar System continuously monitors for potential threats like incoming missiles and measures the coordinates of the targets. It then sends these coordinates to the Control

System, which then determines the level of threat possessed by the target based on the information from the Radar System.

The Command and Decision System then calculates different parameters of the target like speed of the missile, flight path and possible point of impact.

Based on the above parameters, the Control System then activates the Weapons Firing System, which fires continuously until the target is destroyed.

In this example, the communication between the Command and Decision System and the Radar system happens in real time i.e. a potential threat can occur at any time and it is unpredictable. The second real time computing is the firing coordinates. Initially, they are determined by the flight path of the target but are updated in real time as per the actual location of the target.

Characteristics of a Real Time Embedded System

There are two important characteristics of any real time embedded system. They are:

- The Real Time Embedded System must generate correct computational responses to the events (functional constraints) and
- The responses or results must be produced within a predefined time (timing constraints).

Types of Real Time Systems

In the characteristics section, we have said that a real time system must comply with timing constraints. Based on the degree of tolerance in the timing constraints, Real Time Systems are classified in to two types. They are:

- Hard Real Time Systems
- Soft Real Time Systems

In Hard Real Time Systems, there is no flexibility in timing constraints i.e. they must meet all the deadlines, failing to do will result in a catastrophic consequences.

A Hard Real Time System must produce accurate responses to the events within specified time period. If either of them are not achieved i.e. if the response isn't accurate or if the response isn't delivered in right time, the result will be extremely catastrophic, like loss of life.

Examples for Hard Real Time Systems are Flight Control Systems, Missile Guidance Systems, Weapons Defense System, etc.

On the other hand, Soft Real Time Systems have some relaxation in meeting the deadlines i.e. the degree of tolerance is non-zero. A Soft Real Time System must produce response to an event within the deadline but with some flexibility in meeting the deadlines.

Even if the response isn't delivered in the deadline (but delivered in acceptable limit), the result won't be catastrophic or failure in the system but will cost a delay in propagation.

Examples for Soft Real Time Systems are Set top boxes, DVD Players, Weather Monitoring Systems etc.

3.12. Why Real Time Systems Need Operating System?

Operating System is a piece of software that controls different hardware in a system like Processor, Memory and other devices and also provides a user interface for interaction between the user and the system.

In Real Time Systems, where Real Time Computing is required with accurate results that must be delivered on time, Operating System plays an important role. With the increasing complexity of the hardware in Embedded Systems, the features they provide and the applications they can run need an Operating System Code so that it meets the system requirements and also doesn't miss any deadlines.

Small Embedded Systems like Microwave Ovens might not require an Operating System but some advanced systems like Set top Boxes, which can play over a 1000 channels, can record High Definition Videos and support Media from external devices like USB, definitely need an Operating System.

The Operating System used in Real Time Systems is called as Real Time Operating System or RTOS

Real Time Operating System (RTOS)

Real Time Operating System or RTOS manages the resources of a Real Time Embedded System such that any process will take the same amount of time it has taken the previous time. An RTOS should have a predictable response to an unpredictable event.

With the help of RTOS, Real Time Applications can be easily designed and additional functions can be added without any hassle (no additional software is required).

3.13. Example of Embedded System and its Real Time Applications

We will proceed further in to the discussion by looking at an example of an Embedded System and its Real Time Application: Anti-lock Brakes in automobiles.

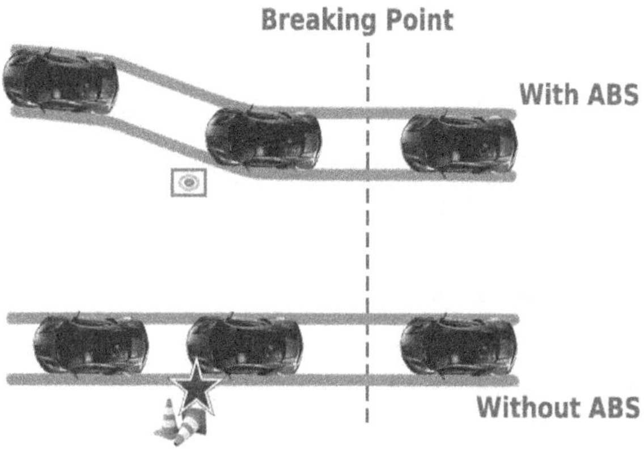

Almost all modern cars (and motor cycles as well) are equipped with a safety feature called Anti – lock Braking System or ABS. What we doesn't know is that it is an embedded system serving a real time application: allowing wheels to have traction with the road and preventing the wheels to lock up and skid when the brakes are applied.

Where is the Real – Time Concept in this example? Let us dig a little deeper. Generally, when we apply brakes on a car, the brake pressure will be applied on all the wheels irrespective of the orientation of the wheel and speed of the car, causing the wheels to lock. This will result in skidding of the vehicle and loss of traction (there is separate Traction control system).

ABS (Anti-locking Barking System) plays an important role in such situations. An ABS system typically comprises of three parts: Sensors, Control Unit and Hydraulic Valves.

Each wheel has its own sensor, which helps in continuously monitoring the speed of rotation of the wheel. The data from the sensor is constantly monitored by the Electronic Control Unit (ECU).

If the rotational speed of a wheel is less than that of the others, the wheel is susceptible to locking when brakes are applied.

The ECU will then activate the hydraulic valves according to the rotational speed of the wheel i.e. less hydraulic pressure to the wheel rotating at slower speed than others. The reduction in hydraulic pressure to the brake will reduce the braking force on that particular wheel and thus all the wheels will be synchronized.

The other case i.e. if the rotational speed of a wheel is higher than the others, then also ABS comes in to picture.

3.14. Some Other Real Time Applications of Embedded Systems

- Latest Smart TVs
- GPS Navigation Systems
- Almost all Modern Day Smart Phones
- Missile Guidance Systems
- Space Exploration (Rovers)
- Automobiles (ABS, Airbags)
- Industries (Assembly Robots)
- Road Safety Systems (Traffic Monitoring and Collision Alert Systems) and many other.

Operating System | Types of Operating Systems

An Operating System performs all the basic tasks like managing file, process, and memory. Thus operating system acts as manager of all the resources, i.e. resource manager. Thus operating system becomes an interface between user and machine.

Types of Operating Systems: Some of the widely used operating systems are as follows-

Batch Operating System

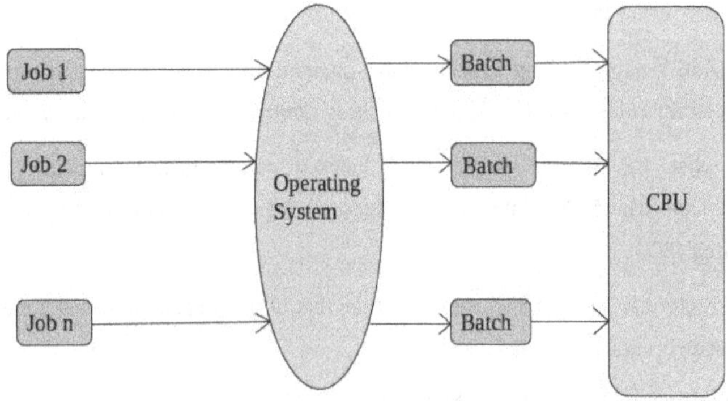

This type of operating system do not interact with the computer directly. There is an operator which takes similar jobs having same requirement and group them into batches. It is the responsibility of operator to sort the jobs with similar needs.

Advantages of Batch Operating System

It is very difficult to guess or know the time required by any job to complete. Processors of the batch systems knows how long the job would be when it is in queue.

Multiple users can share the batch systems.

The idle time batch system is very less.

It is easy to manage large work repeatedly in batch systems.

Disadvantages of Batch Operating System

The computer operators should be well known with batch systems.

Batch systems are hard to debug.

It is sometime costly.

The other jobs will have to wait for an unknown time if any job fails

Examples of Batch based Operating System: Payroll System, Bank Statements etc.

Time-Sharing Operating Systems

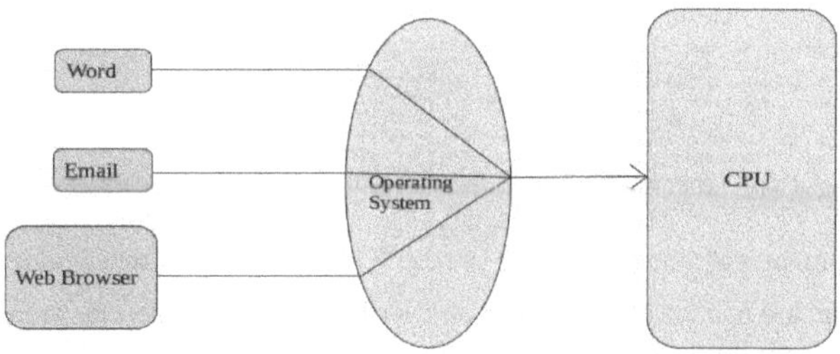

Each task has given some time to execute, so that all the tasks work smoothly. Each user gets time of CPU as they use single system. These systems are also known as Multitasking Systems. The task can be from single user or from different users also. The time that each task gets to execute is called quantum. After this time interval is over OS switches over to next task.

Advantages of Time-Sharing OS

Each task gets an equal opportunity.

Less chances of duplication of software.

CPU idle time can be reduced.

Disadvantages of Time-Sharing OS

Reliability problem.

One must have to take care of security and integrity of user programs and data.

Data communication problem.

Examples of Time-Sharing OSs are: Multics, Unix etc.

Distributed Operating System

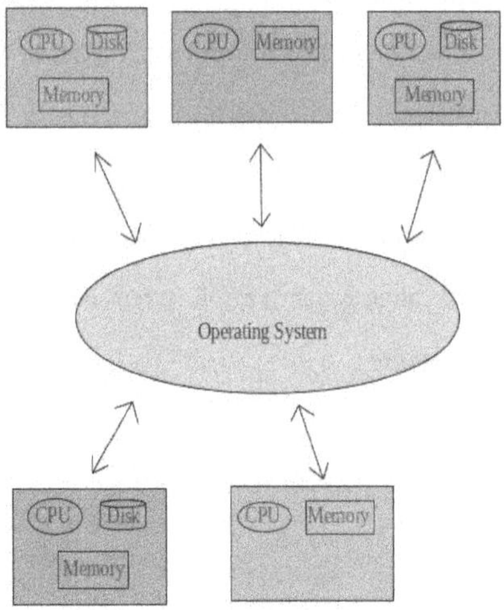

These types of operating system is a recent advancement in the world of computer technology and are being widely accepted all-over the world and, that too, with a great pace. Various autonomous interconnected computers communicate each other using a shared communication network. Independent systems possess their own memory unit and CPU. These are referred as loosely coupled systems or distributed systems. These systems processors differ in sizes and functions. The major benefit of working with these types of operating system is that it is always possible that one user can access the files or software which are not actually present on his system but on some other system connected within this network i.e., remote access is enabled within the devices connected in that network.

Advantages of Distributed Operating System

Failure of one will not affect the other network communication, as all systems are independent from each other.

Electronic mail increases the data exchange speed.

Since resources are being shared, computation is highly fast and durable.

Load on host computer reduces.

These systems are easily scalable as many systems can be easily added to the network.

Delay in data processing reduces.

Disadvantages of Distributed Operating System

Failure of the main network will stop the entire communication.

To establish distributed systems the language which are used are not well defined yet.

These types of systems are not readily available as they are very expensive. Not only that the underlying software is highly complex and not understood well yet.

Examples of Distributed Operating System are- LOCUS etc.

Network Operating System

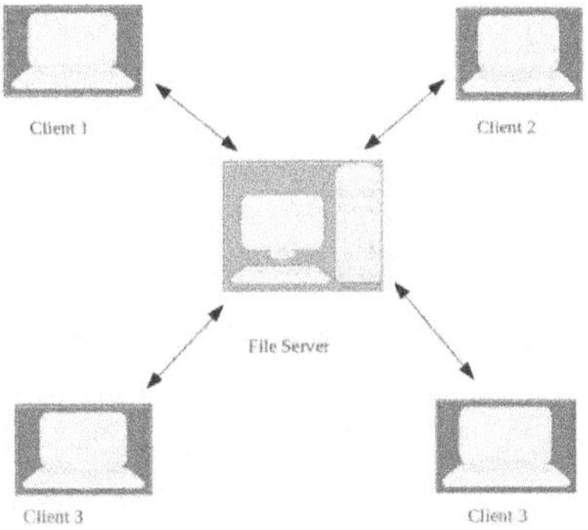

These systems runs on a server and provides the capability to manage data, users, groups, security, applications, and other networking functions. These type of operating systems allows shared access of files, printers, security, applications, and other networking functions over a small private network. One more important aspect of Network Operating Systems is that all the users are well aware of the underlying configuration, of all other users within the network, their individual connections etc. and that's why these computers are popularly known as tightly coupled systems.

Advantages of Network Operating System

Highly stable centralized servers.

Security concerns are handled through servers.

New technologies and hardware up-gradation are easily integrated to the system.

Server access are possible remotely from different locations and types of systems.

Disadvantages of Network Operating System

Servers are costly.

User has to depend on central location for most operations.

Maintenance and updates are required regularly.

Examples of Network Operating System are: Microsoft Windows Server 2003, Microsoft Windows Server 2008, UNIX, Linux, Mac OS X, Novell NetWare, and BSD etc.

Real-Time Operating System

These types of OSs serves the real-time systems. The time interval required to process and respond to inputs is very small. This time interval is called response time.

Real-time systems are used when there are time requirements are very strict like missile systems, air traffic control systems, robots etc.

Two Types of Real-Time Operating System Which Are as Follows.

Hard Real-Time Systems

These OSs are meant for the applications where time constraints are very strict and even the shortest possible delay is not acceptable. These systems are built for saving life like automatic parachutes or air bags which are required to be readily available in case of any accident. Virtual memory is almost never found in these systems.

Soft Real-Time Systems

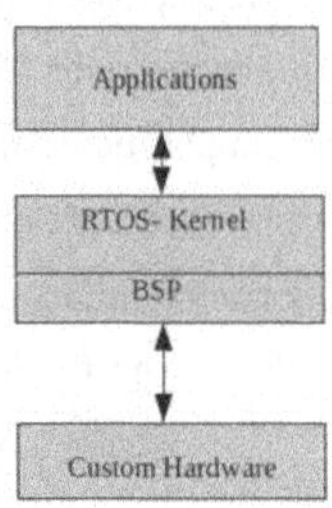

These OSs are for applications where for time-constraint is less strict.

Advantages of RTOS

Maximum Consumption: Maximum utilization of devices and system, thus more output from all the resources

Task Shifting: Time assigned for shifting tasks in these systems are very less. For example in older systems it takes about 10 micro seconds in shifting one task to another and in latest systems it takes 3 micro seconds.

Focus on Application: Focus on running applications and less importance to applications which are in queue.

Real time operating system in embedded system: Since size of programs are small, RTOS can also be used in embedded systems like in transport and others.

Error Free: These types of systems are error free.

Memory Allocation: Memory allocation is best managed in these type of systems.

Disadvantages of RTOS

Limited Tasks: Very few task run at the same time and their concentration is very less on few applications to avoid errors.

Use heavy system resources: Sometimes the system resources are not so good and they are expensive as well.

Complex Algorithms: The algorithms are very complex and difficult for the designer to write on.

Device driver and interrupt signals: It needs specific device drivers and interrupt signals to response earliest to interrupts.

Thread Priority: It is not good to set thread priority as these systems are very less pron to switching tasks.

Examples of Real-Time Operating Systems are: Scientific experiments, medical imaging systems, industrial control systems, weapon systems, robots, air traffic control systems, etc.

Types of Operating System

Operating systems are there from the very first computer generation and they keep evolving with time. In this chapter, we will discuss some of the important types of operating systems which are most commonly used.

Batch Operating System

The users of a batch operating system do not interact with the computer directly. Each user prepares his job on an off-line device like punch cards and submits it to the computer operator. To speed up processing, jobs with similar needs are batched together and run as a group. The programmers leave their programs with the operator and the operator then sorts the programs with similar requirements into batches.

The problems with Batch Systems are as follows.

Lack of interaction between the user and the job.

CPU is often idle, because the speed of the mechanical I/O devices is slower than the CPU.

Difficult to provide the desired priority.

Time-Sharing Operating Systems

Time-sharing is a technique which enables many people, located at various terminals, to use a particular computer system at the same time. Time-sharing or multitasking is a logical extension of multiprogramming. Processor's time which is shared among multiple users simultaneously is termed as time-sharing.

The main difference between Multiprogrammed Batch Systems and Time-Sharing Systems is that in case of Multiprogrammed batch systems, the objective is to maximize processor use, whereas in Time-Sharing Systems, the objective is to minimize response time.

Multiple jobs are executed by the CPU by switching between them, but the switches occur so frequently. Thus, the user can receive an immediate response. For example, in a transaction processing, the processor executes each user program in a short burst or quantum of computation. That is, if n users are present, then each user can get a time quantum. When the user submits the command, the response time is in few seconds at most.

The operating system uses CPU scheduling and multiprogramming to provide each user with a small portion of a time. Computer systems that were designed primarily as batch systems have been modified to time-sharing systems.

Advantages of Timesharing operating systems are as follows.

Provides the advantage of quick response.

Avoids duplication of software.

Reduces CPU idle time.

Disadvantages of Time-sharing operating systems are as follows.

Problem of reliability.

Question of security and integrity of user programs and data.

Problem of data communication.

Distributed Operating System

Distributed systems use multiple central processors to serve multiple real-time applications and multiple users. Data processing jobs are distributed among the processors accordingly.

The processors communicate with one another through various communication lines (such as high-speed buses or telephone lines). These are referred as loosely coupled systems or distributed systems. Processors in a distributed system may vary in size and function. These processors are referred as sites, nodes, computers, and so on.

The advantages of distributed systems are as follows.

With resource sharing facility, a user at one site may be able to use the resources available at another.

Speedup the exchange of data with one another via electronic mail.

If one site fails in a distributed system, the remaining sites can potentially continue operating.

Better service to the customers.

Reduction of the load on the host computer.

Reduction of delays in data processing.

Network Operating System

A Network Operating System runs on a server and provides the server the capability to manage data, users, groups, security, applications, and other networking functions. The primary purpose of the network operating system is to allow shared file and printer access among multiple computers in a network, typically a local area network (LAN), a private network or to other networks.

Examples of network operating systems include Microsoft Windows Server 2003, Microsoft Windows Server 2008, UNIX, Linux, Mac OS X, Novell NetWare, and BSD.

The advantages of network operating systems are as follows.

Centralized servers are highly stable.

Security is server managed.

Upgrades to new technologies and hardware can be easily integrated into the system.

Remote access to servers is possible from different locations and types of systems.

The disadvantages of network operating systems are as follows.

High cost of buying and running a server.

Dependency on a central location for most operations.

Regular maintenance and updates are required.

Real Time Operating System

A real-time system is defined as a data processing system in which the time interval required to process and respond to inputs is so small that it controls the environment. The time taken by the system to respond to an input and display of required updated information is termed as the response time. So in this method, the response time is very less as compared to online processing.

Real-time systems are used when there are rigid time requirements on the operation of a processor or the flow of data and real-time systems can be used as a control device in a dedicated application. A real-time operating system must have well-defined, fixed time constraints, otherwise the system will fail. For example, Scientific experiments, medical imaging systems, industrial control systems, weapon systems, robots, air traffic control systems, etc.

There are Two Types of Real-Time Operating Systems

Hard Real-Time Systems

Hard real-time systems guarantee that critical tasks complete on time. In hard real-time systems, secondary storage is limited or missing and the data is stored in ROM. In these systems, virtual memory is almost never found.

Soft Real-Time Systems

Soft real-time systems are less restrictive. A critical real-time task gets priority over other tasks and retains the priority until it completes. Soft real-time systems have limited utility than hard real-time systems.

For example, multimedia, virtual reality, Advanced Scientific Projects like undersea exploration and planetary rovers, etc.

Processes and Threads

A process is an instance of program execution. This means, for example, that if you open up two browser windows then you have two processes, even though they are running the same program.

The life-cycle of a process can be described by a state diagram which has states representing the execution status of the process at various times and transitions that represent changes in execution status.

The operating system maintains management information about a process in a process control block (PCB). Modern operating systems allow a process to be divided into multiple threads of execution, which share all process management information except for information directly related to execution. This information is held in a thread control block (TCB).

Threads in a process can execute different parts of the program code at the same time. They can also execute the same parts of the code at the same time, but with different execution state:

They have independent current instructions; that is, they have (or appear to have) independent program counters.

They are working with different data; that is, they are (or appear to be) working with independent registers.

State Diagram

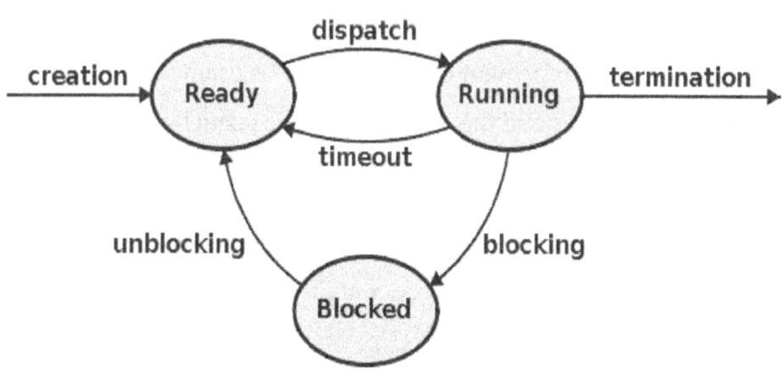

The state diagram for a process captures its life-cycle. The states represent the execution status of the process; the transitions represent changes of execution state.

Each active process has its own execution status, so there is a state diagram for each process. There are relationships between the states of various processes that are maintained by the operating system.

States

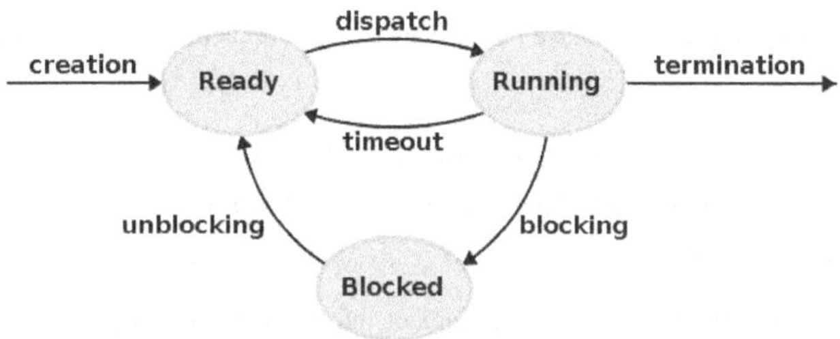

The state of a process represent its execution status.

Transitions

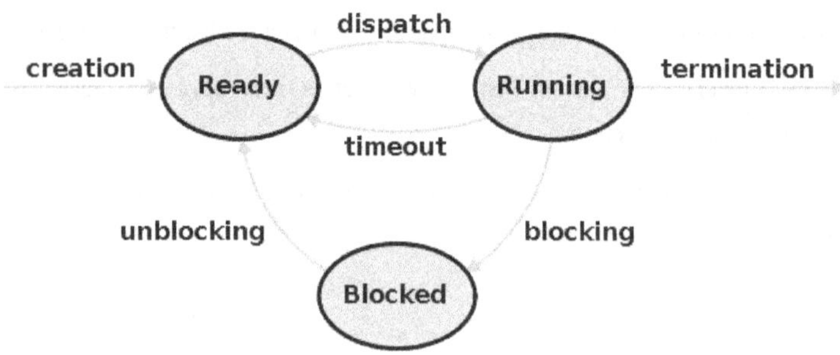

The transitions of a process represent changes of its execution state. The transitions can be described in terms of their causes and the resulting actions taken by the operating system.

Process Control Block

An operating system maintains a structure called a process control block (PCB) for each of its active processes. The PCB for a process contains or refers to the following kinds of information.

Resource management information administrative information an execution snapshot

3.15. Thread Fork

A thread fork operation behaves like a function call. It creates a new child thread whose execution snapshot is identical to the parent thread's snapshot except for the register that contains the function return value. For the child thread the return value is 0; for the parent the return value is the child thread's thread identifier.

Normally, the return value is used in the condition of an if-else statement. If the return value is 0 then child code is executed; otherwise, parent code is executed.

At the system call level, a thread fork operation involves saving a new execution snapshot for the parent thread in its TCB creating a new TCB whose execution snapshot is identical to the parent's execution snapshot changing the return value register in the two snapshots The operating system then has the option of dispatching the child, putting the parent in the ready queue, or dispatching the parent, putting the child in the ready queue, or putting both the child and the parent in the ready queue, scheduling and dispatching a different thread.

Thread Control Block

A thread control block (TCB) contains a thread identifier, a reference to the PCB for the process to which it belongs, a reference to the TCB for the thread that created it, and an execution snapshot.

A thread has indirect access to non-execution related resources through the PCB of the process to which it belongs. Thus threads within a process share memory, open files, and I/O streams.

3.16. Operating System - Multi-Threading

What is Thread?

A thread is a flow of execution through the process code, with its own program counter that keeps track of which instruction to execute next, system registers which hold its current working variables, and a stack which contains the execution history.

A thread shares with its peer threads few information like code segment, data segment and open files. When one thread alters a code segment memory item, all other threads see that.

A thread is also called a lightweight process. Threads provide a way to improve application performance through parallelism. Threads represent a software approach to improving performance of operating system by reducing the overhead thread is equivalent to a classical process.

Each thread belongs to exactly one process and no thread can exist outside a process. Each thread represents a separate flow of control. Threads have been successfully used in implementing network servers and web server. They also provide a suitable foundation for parallel execution of applications on shared memory multiprocessors. The following figure shows the working of a single-threaded and a multithreaded process.

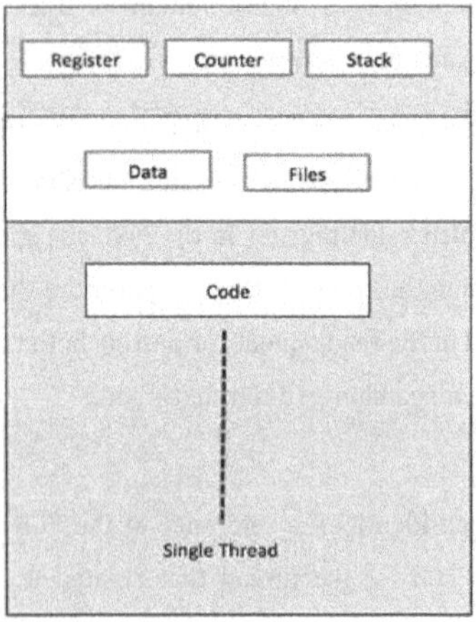

Single Process P with single thread

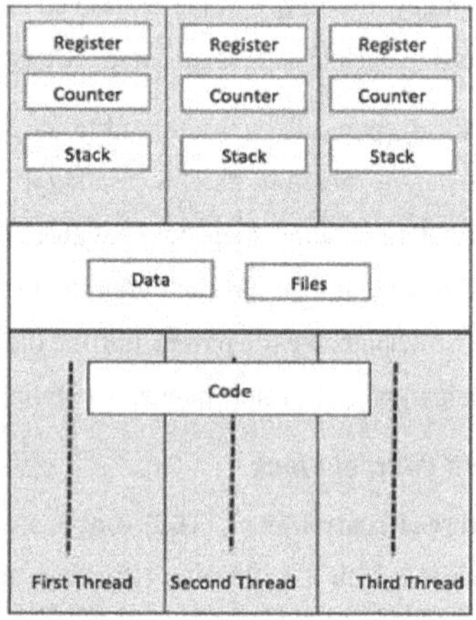

Single Process P with three threads

3.17. Difference between Process and Thread

S.N.	Process	Thread
1	Process is heavy weight or resource intensive.	Thread is light weight, taking lesser resources than a process.
2	Process switching needs interaction with operating system.	Thread switching does not need to interact with operating system.
3	In multiple processing environments, each process executes the same code but has its own memory and file resources.	All threads can share same set of open files, child processes.
4	If one process is blocked, then no other process can execute until the first process is unblocked.	While one thread is blocked and waiting, a second thread in the same task can run.
5	Multiple processes without using threads use more resources.	Multiple threaded processes use fewer resources.
6	In multiple processes each process operates independently of the others.	One thread can read, write or change another thread's data.

Advantages of Thread

- Threads minimize the context switching time.
- Use of threads provides concurrency within a process.
- Efficient communication.
- It is more economical to create and context switch threads.
- Threads allow utilization of multiprocessor architectures to a greater scale and efficiency.

Types of Thread

Threads are implemented in following two ways –

- User Level Threads – User managed threads.
- Kernel Level Threads – Operating System managed threads acting on kernel, an operating system core.

User Level Threads

In this case, the thread management kernel is not aware of the existence of threads. The thread library contains code for creating and destroying threads, for passing message and data between threads, for scheduling thread execution and for saving and restoring thread contexts. The application starts with a single thread.

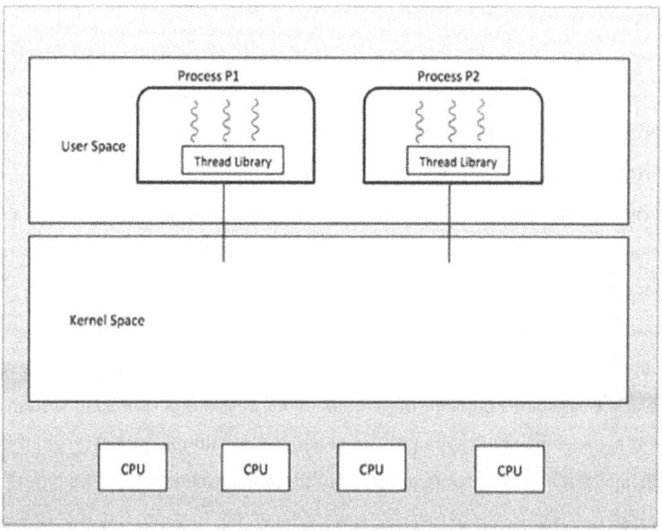

Advantages

- Thread switching does not require Kernel mode privileges.
- User level thread can run on any operating system.
- Scheduling can be application specific in the user level thread.
- User level threads are fast to create and manage.

Disadvantages

- In a typical operating system, most system calls are blocking.
- Multithreaded application cannot take advantage of multiprocessing.
- Kernel Level Threads.

In this case, thread management is done by the Kernel. There is no thread management code in the application area. Kernel threads are supported directly by the operating system. Any application can be programmed to be multithreaded. All of the threads within an application are supported within a single process.

The Kernel maintains context information for the process as a whole and for individuals threads within the process. Scheduling by the Kernel is done on a thread basis. The Kernel performs thread creation, scheduling and management in Kernel space. Kernel threads are generally slower to create and manage than the user threads.

Advantages

- Kernel can simultaneously schedule multiple threads from the same process on multiple processes.
- If one thread in a process is blocked, the Kernel can schedule another thread of the same process.
- Kernel routines themselves can be multithreaded.

Disadvantages

- Kernel threads are generally slower to create and manage than the user threads.
- Transfer of control from one thread to another within the same process requires a mode switch to the Kernel.

Multithreading Models

Some operating system provide a combined user level thread and Kernel level thread facility. Solaris is a good example of this combined approach. In a combined system, multiple threads within the same application can run in parallel on multiple processors and a blocking system call need not block the entire process. Multithreading models are three types.

- Many to many relationship.
- Many to one relationship.
- One to one relationship.

Many to Many Model

The many-to-many model multiplexes any number of user threads onto an equal or smaller number of kernel threads.

The following diagram shows the many-to-many threading model where 6 user level threads are multiplexing with 6 kernel level threads. In this model, developers can create as many user threads as necessary and the corresponding Kernel threads can run in parallel on a multiprocessor machine. This model provides the best accuracy on concurrency and when a thread performs a blocking system call, the kernel can schedule another thread for execution.

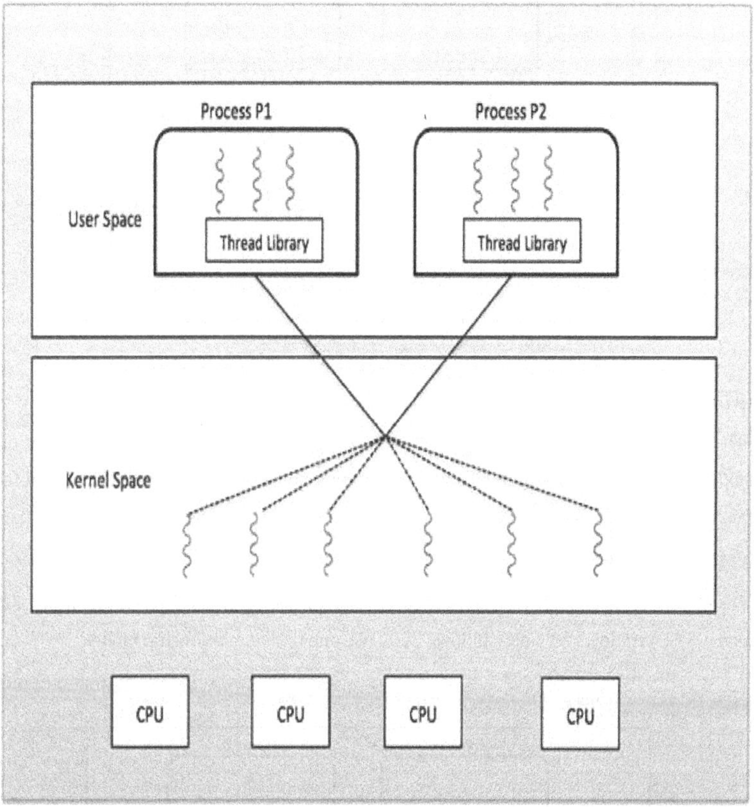

Many to One Model

Many-to-one model maps many user level threads to one Kernel-level thread. Thread management is done in user space by the thread library. When thread makes a blocking system call, the entire process will be blocked. Only one thread can access the Kernel at a time, so multiple threads are unable to run in parallel on multiprocessors.

If the user-level thread libraries are implemented in the operating system in such a way that the system does not support them, then the Kernel threads use the many-to-one relationship modes.

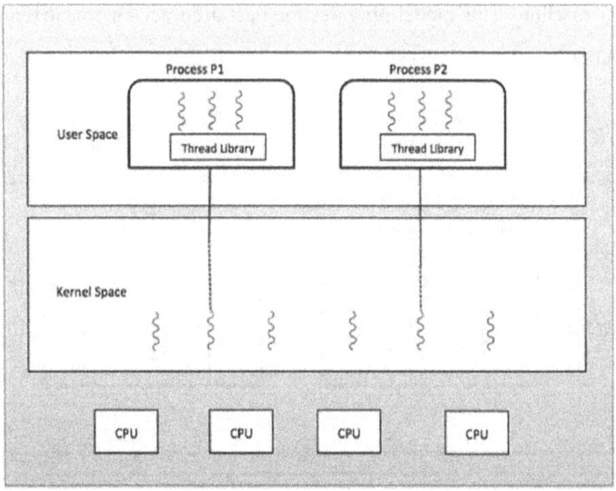

One to One Model

There is one-to-one relationship of user-level thread to the kernel-level thread. This model provides more concurrency than the many-to-one model. It also allows another thread to run when a thread makes a blocking system call. It supports multiple threads to execute in parallel on microprocessors.

Disadvantage of this model is that creating user thread requires the corresponding Kernel thread. OS/2, Windows NT and windows 2000 use one to one relationship model.

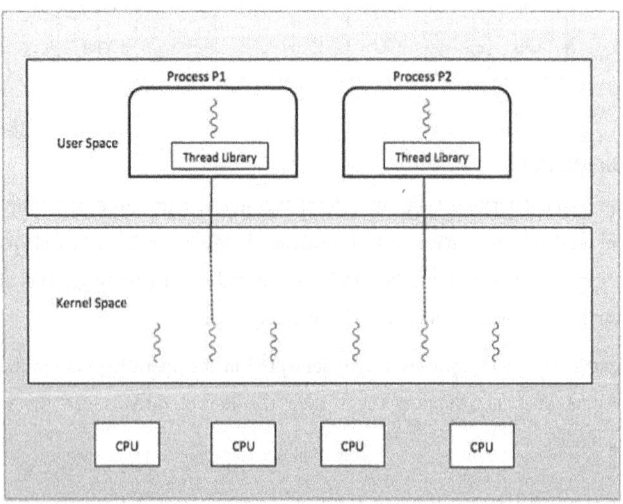

3.18. Difference between User-Level & Kernel-Level Thread

S.N.	User-Level Threads	Kernel-Level Thread
1	User-level threads are faster to create and manage.	Kernel-level threads are slower to create and manage.
2	Implementation is by a thread library at the user level.	Operating system supports creation of Kernel threads.
3	User-level thread is generic and can run on any operating system.	Kernel-level thread is specific to the operating system.
4	Multi-threaded applications cannot take advantage of multiprocessing.	Kernel routines themselves can be multithreaded.

Multiprogramming: More than one task/program/job/process can reside into the *main memory* at one point of time. This ability of the OS is called multiprogramming.

Multitasking: More than one task/program/job/process can reside into the *same CPU* at one point of time. This ability of the OS is called multitasking.

16.

None of the above answers except Mr Vaibhav Kumar's are clear or not ambiguous. [sorry, no offense]

Both multi programming and tasking are same concept of switching task in processor, difference is in the concept and reason of the switching.

MProgramming: to not keep processor idle when active task needs longer IO or other non CPU response then, processor loads and works on another task that is not waiting for IO and ready for **process.**

MTasking: even after MPrograming, to user it may feel like only one task is executing and another is simply waiting to come to cpu. So the active task is also swapped from active CPU and kept aside and another task is brought in CPU for a very small fraction of human time [second], and swapped back to the earlier task again. In this way user will feel both task are alive in CPU at same time. But actually each task is active only once at a given CPU time[in micro or nano second]

And MProcessing is, like my computer have quad core, so I use 4 processor at a time, means 4 different multiprogramming instances happen in my machine. And these 4 processors does another numerous no of MTasking.

So M Processing>M Programming>Mtasking and M Threading n another breakup of each task. that also to give user a happy life. Here multiple tasks[like word doc and media player] are not coming in picture, rather small subtasks like coloring of text on word and automatic spell check in word are part of same word executable.

Multiprogramming: It means running several programs on computer. Here user cannot interact with the system, everything is decided by the OS.

Multitasking: It is a logical extension of multiprogramming. It means running several tasks on computer. Switching between the jobs is so fast that the user can interact with the system.

Multithreading: Basically seen when more number of clients access the server.

Multiprogramming- Jobs to be executed are loaded into a pool. Some number of those jobs are loaded into main memory, and one is selected from the pool for execution by the CPU. If at some point the program in progress terminates or requires the services of a peripheral device, the control of the CPU is given to the next job in the pool. As programs terminate, more jobs are loaded into memory for execution, and CPU control is switched to another job in memory. In this way the CPU is always executing some program or some portion thereof, instead of waiting for a printer, tape drive, or console input

Multiprocessing - the simultaneous execution of two or more programs or instruction sequences by separate CPUs under integrated control

Multitasking System - the concurrent or interleaved execution of two or more jobs by a single **CPU.**

Multi users System - a computer system in which multiple terminals connect to a host computer that handles processing tasks.

Multiprogramming and multitasking; both solve different problems, though they use similar method of switching between processes.

Multiprogramming: It was seen in early days that certain processes at times need to use peripherals (e.g.: I/O), in which cases the CPU remained idle. To use the CPU more efficiently it was thought of having multiple processes in the memory so that if a certain process being executed needs a peripheral, certain other process might use the CPU. This was the idea behind multiprogramming.

Multitasking: It is required that multiple process should appear to be running at the same time to the end user. So that is mocked by switching between these processes and by making them run on the CPU simultaneously. This is multitasking.

UNIT 4

CHARACTERISTICS AND QUALITY ATTRIBUTES OF EMBEDDED SYSTEMS

4.1. Objectives

After reading this chapter you will:

Understand the characteristics of Embedded system

Understand the attributes related to quality of embedded system.

4.2. Introduction

The characteristics of embedded system are different from those of a general purpose computer and so are its Quality metrics. This chapter gives a brief introduction on the characteristics of an embedded system and the attributes that are associated with its quality.

4.3. Characteristics of Embedded System

Following are some of the characteristics of an embedded system that make it different from a general purpose computer:

Application and Domain Specific

An embedded system is designed for a specific purpose only. It will not do any other task.

Ex. A washing machine can only wash, it cannot cook.

Certain embedded systems are specific to a domain: ex. A hearing aid is an application that belongs to the domain of signal processing.

Reactive and Real Time

Certain Embedded systems are designed to react to the events that occur in the nearby environment. These events also occur real-time.

Ex. An air conditioner adjusts its mechanical parts as soon as it gets a signal from its sensors to increase or decrease the temperature when the user operates it using a remote control. An embedded system uses Sensors to take inputs and has actuators to bring out the required functionality.

Operation in Harsh Environment

Certain embedded systems are designed to operate in harsh environments like very high temperature of the deserts or very low temperature of the mountains or extreme rains.

These embedded systems have to be capable of sustaining the environmental conditions it is designed to operate in.

Distributed

Certain embedded systems are part of a larger system and thus form components of a distributed system.

These components are independent of each other but have to work together for the larger system to function properly.

Ex. A car has many embedded systems controlled to its dash board. Each one is an independent embedded system yet the entire car can be said to function properly only if all the systems work together.

Small Size and Weight

An embedded system that is compact in size and has light weight will be desirable or more popular than one that is bulky and heavy.

Ex. Currently available cell phones. The cell phones that have the maximum features are popular but also their size and weight is an important characteristic.

For convenience users prefer mobile phones than phablets. (phone + tablet pc)

Power Concerns

It is desirable that the power utilization and heat dissipation of any embedded system be low.

If more heat is dissipated then additional units like heat sinks or cooling fans need to be added to the circuit.

If more power is required then a battery of higher power or more batteries need to be accommodated in the embedded system.

Let's see the general characteristics of embedded system in the real-time computation of system:

1. An embedded system is software embedded into computer hardware that makes a system dedicated to be used for variety of application.
2. Embedded system generally used for do specific task that provide real-time output on the basis of various characteristics of an embedded system.

3. Embedded system may contain a smaller part within a larger device that used for serving the more specific application to perform variety of task using hardware-software intermixing configuration.
4. It provides high reliability and real-time computation ability.

Let's See the Characteristics of Hardware and Software Interfacing in the Real World of Embedded Systems

S. No	Software Interface	Hardware Interface	Visual Aid	Remarks
1	Driver for LED	Session: Interfacing of Display Diagram: Interfacing of LED	LED glowing On and Off.	Handling a single segment in 7 segment display as a single LED
2	Driver for 7 segment display	Session: Interfacing of Display Diagram 1: Interfacing of single 7 segment display Diagram 2: Interfacing of multiple 7 segment display	Displaying numbers 0000 to 9999 on 7-segment display.	Simple multiplexing without the use of Display Look up Table. Static display
3	Driver for multiplexing 4 seven segment displays	Session: Interfacing of Display Diagram 1: Interfacing of single 7 segment display Diagram 2: Interfacing of multiple 7 segment displays	Displaying numbers 0000 to 9999 on 7-segment display.	Multiplexing of 7 segment display taking patterns from Display Look up Table.
4	Counter	Application on seven-segment display.	Showing continuously incrementing values on seven-segment display	Without interrupt, Without ASCII values
5	Counter	Application on seven-segment display.	Showing continuously incrementing values on seven-segment display	Without interrupt, With ASCII values
6	Timer Counter	Session: Time / Counter initialization.	Blinking LED	Timer in Polling mode
Concept of background and foreground process for I/O handling using Interrupt				
7	Generating Timer Interrupt	Session: Timer and interrupt structure Diagram 1: Timer SFR Diagram2: Interrupt Vector Table	Blinking of dot on seven-segment display.	Dot indicates occurrence of interrupt
8	Interrupt based display driver for seven segment display	Session: timer and interrupt structure Diagram 1: 1ms interrupt structure Diagram 2: Scanner program flow chart	Four digit counter application on seven-segment display	With interrupt, with ASCII values
9	Interrupt based hex key pad driver	Session: Interfacing of keys Diagram1: Interfacing of Key Diagram 2: Interfacing of Hex Key pad, Scan lines and Return lines Diagram 3: Scanner program flow chart	Displaying the value of key pressed till user presses another key	Key pad scanning with interrupt
10	Complete Stopwatch application	Related to each of the above	Showing continuously incrementing values on seven-segment display	A key for starting SW B key for stopping SW C key for resetting SW

Advantages

- Same hardware can be used in variety of application.
- Lesser power requirement
- Lower operational cost of system
- Provide high performance and efficiency

Disadvantages

- Developing a system required more time. Due to functional complexity.
- EMBEDDED SYSTEMS BASICS: **Embedded system** is described as a manner of running, acting or organizing one or many tasks in keeping with a set of rules (or) an association in which all the devices collect and paintings collectively in step with the program or plan. **Examples of embedded**_structures are an eye and washing system.

Embedded Systems Basics, Characteristics and Applications Microcontrollers

EMBEDDED SYSTEMS BASICS: Embedded system is described as a manner of running, acting or organizing one or many tasks in keeping with a set of rules (or) an association in which all the devices collect and paintings collectively in step with the program or plan. Examples of embedded structures are an eye and washing system.

An embedded device is a machine that has software program embedded in PC hardware. It makes a device devoted to a selected a part of an application or fabricated from a bigger device. Depending on the application, embedded device can be programmable or non-programmable. Examples of embedded systems consist of diverse merchandise together with washing system, microwave ovens, cameras, printers, and motors. You can check the application of embedded systems in the medical field.

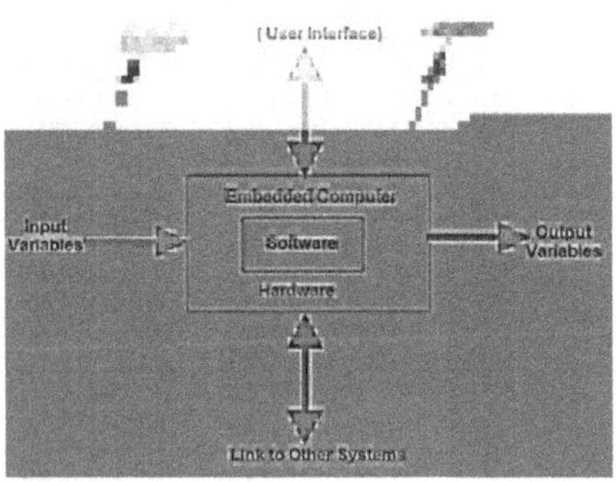

Figure 1: Embedded System

They use microprocessors and microcontrollers in addition to specially designed processors consisting of digital signal processors (DSP).

Figure 2: Block Diagram OF Embedded System

Embedded Systems Hardware

As with every electronic device, an embedded device calls for a hardware platform in which it plays the operation. Embedded device hardware is built with a microprocessor or microcontroller. The embedded device hardware has factors like entering output (I/O) interfaces, consumer interface, reminiscence and the display. Usually, an embedded system consists of:

- Power supply
- Processor
- Timers
- Serial exchange ports
- Input/output circuits
- System service specific circuits

In some instances, customized chips may be feasible for a particular utility if quantities are sufficiently high. One common example of a popular elegance of devoted processor is the virtual signal processor, DSP. This type of processor is used for processing audio and photo files especially. Processing is required in no time as they may be utilized in packages which include mobile telephones and the like.

Embedded System Software

The embedded device software is written to carry out a selected feature. It is commonly written in a high degree format after which compiled right down to provide code that can be lodged inside a non-risky reminiscence within the hardware. An embedded gadget software program is designed to keep in view of the 3 limits:

- Availability of machine memory
- Availability of processor's speed
- When the system runs continuously, there may be a want to limit power dissipation for events like prevent, run and wake up.

Real Time Operating System

A device is said to be actual time if it's miles vital to complete its work and supply its service on time. Actual time running system manages the software and provides a mechanism to let the processor run. The actual time operating gadget is accountable for handling the hardware sources of a computer and host programs which run on the PC.

An RTOS is in particular designed to run applications with very particular timing and an excessive quantity of reliability. Specifically, this can be important in size and commercial automation systems wherein downtime is highly-priced or an application postpones should reason a protection chance.

Memory

In an embedded gadget, there are special kinds of memories. The extraordinary varieties of processors utilized in an embedded system consisting of digital signal processor (DSP), microprocessor, RISC processor, microcontroller, ASSP processor, ASIP processor.

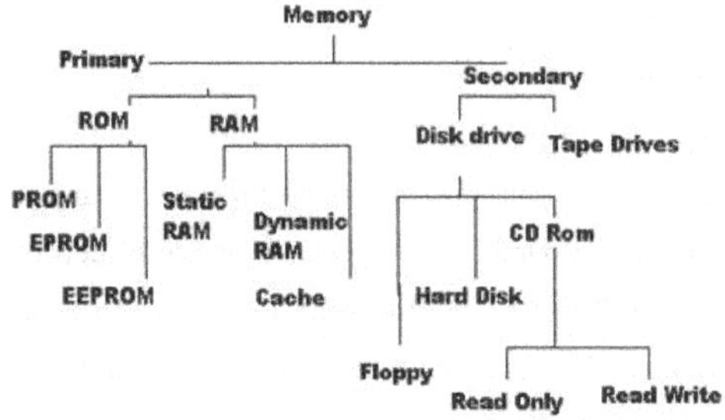

Introduction to arm based LPC 2148 Microcontroller: LPC 2148 microcontroller belongs to ARM7 (Advanced RISC Machine) family, means the ARM is basically an architecture that is used in microcontroller and processors. The word RISC stands for reduced instruction set computer, as its name shows that it is just like a small or mini controller which works on the basis of less instruction as compared to other conventional microcontrollers. This LPC 2148 microcontroller used the 16-bit/32-bit set instruction architecture for real time emulation. It also contains the embedded trace support for combing the microcontroller to high speed flash memory whose ranging between 32KB to 512kB. Its unique accelerator architecture structure and 128kB wide memory enables the code execution at high clock rate.

ARM based LPC 2148 Microcontroller Architecture Microcontrollers Lab 17 Hours Ago No Comments.

Introduction to arm based LPC 2148 Microcontroller: LPC 2148 microcontroller belongs to ARM7 (Advanced RISC Machine) family, means the ARM is basically an architecture that is used in microcontroller and processors. The word RISC stands for reduced instruction set computer, as its name shows that it is just like a small or mini controller which works on the basis of less instruction as compared to other conventional microcontrollers. This LPC 2148 microcontroller used the 16-bit/32-bit set instruction architecture for real time emulation. It also contains the embedded trace support for combing the microcontroller to high speed flash memory whose ranging between 32KB to 512kB. Its unique accelerator architecture structure and 128kB wide memory enables the code execution at high clock rate.

ARM is a company now which manufactures microcontroller and microprocessors for various types of mobiles, iphones and digital devices. ARM is among the most popular processor companies. It is used in maximum mobile phone of the world. ARM processors are power efficient which makes them suitable for low power embedded applications. Therefore ARM based microcontroller or microprocessors are used in mostly embedded applications now a days. LPC2148 microcontroller has ARM 7 based architecture.

General Features of LPC2148 Microcontroller

This ARM microcontroller is best for critical code size applications because it can easily reduce the code size to 30% without reducing the performance. They are easily available in tiny size and consume less power as compared to other microcontrollers. So, due to tiny size and consume less power, these microcontrollers are ideal for that applications where miniaturization is major requirements such as at point of sale and access control etc. It consists of serial communication interface whose ranging from a USB 2, full speed device, multiple

UARTs, SPI, SSP to 12C bus and 8kB to, up to 40 kB no chip SRAM, all these features are so much appropriate for communication gateway and protocol converters. Beside this, it also consists of various 32 bit timers,10 bit DAC (Digital to analog converter),10 bit ADC (analog to digital converter) ,PWM(pulse width modulation) channel,45 fast GPIO lines and level sensitive external interrupts pins make this microcontroller very special for medical system and industrial controls. The general architecture block diagram of this LPC 2148 microcontroller with all their essential parts is shown in figure 3.

General Architecture Block Diagram of LPC 2148 Microcontroller.

Here is the general architecture block diagram of LPC 2148 microcontroller with all their essential parts, LPC 2148 ARM7 Microcontroller Architecture.

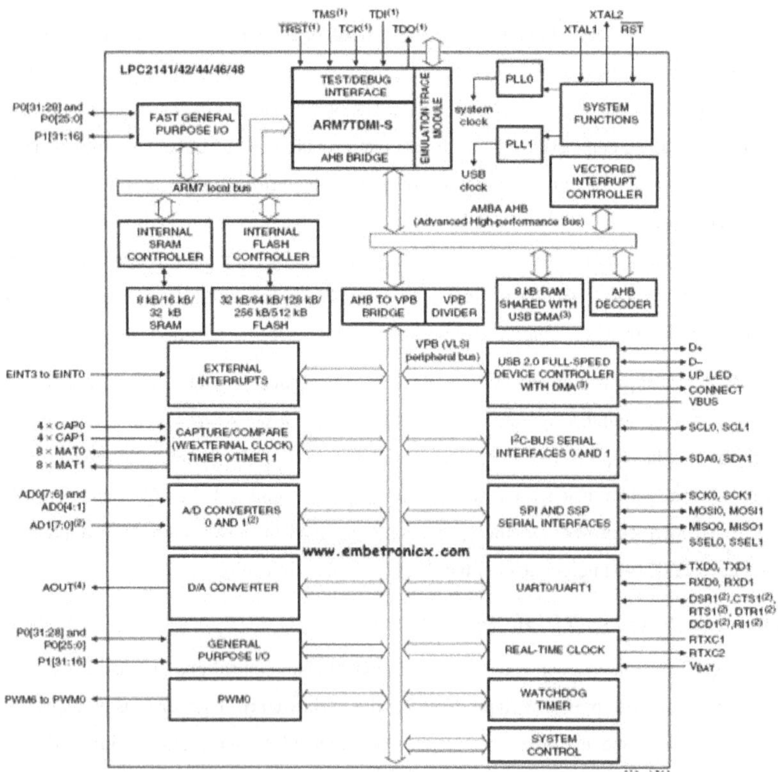

Figure 3: General Architecture Block Diagram of LPC 2148 Microcontroller with all their Essential Parts

Description about General Architecture of LPC 2148 Microcontroller

LPC 2148 microcontroller consist of three buses such as ARM7 Local bus, AHB (Advanced high performance bus) and VPB bus etc. these buses are used for performing different function and these are also consisting of different functioning parts such as ,

GPIO pins: ARM based LPC2148 microcontroller has 45 general purpose input output pins. The operating voltage of these input output pins is 5 volt.

On Chip Static RAM (SRAM): This on chip static ram is used for storing data or code. This ram could be accessed as 8 bit,16 bit or 32 bit. The memory of this ram could be increased to 8 kB,16 kB or 32 kB by using USB.

On Chip Flash Program Memory: LPC 2148 microcontroller contains 512 kB on chip flash memory this memory is used for almost data storage or code storage. The programming of this flash memory could be accomplished with several ways.

Vectored Interrupt Controller: All input requests are received by vectored interrupt controller (VIC) and it converts them into fast interrupt request (FIQ). So, fast interrupt request and non fast interrupt requests are defined by programming setting in vectored interrupt controller.

Digital to analog Converter: This LPC 2148 microcontroller has one 10 bit digital to analog converter (DAC).This converter converts the digital input into analog output. The maximum DAC output voltages are called VREF voltages. Power down mode and buffered output is also available in this digital to analog converter.

Analog to Digital Converter: This LPC 2148 microcontroller also contains two analog to digital converters whose names are ADC0 and ADC0. There are 14 total number of inputs of ADC are available and these two converters successfully converts 10 bit analog input to digital output. The measurement rang of each convert is 0V to VREF and global star command is used for both converters.

UART: This LPC 2148 microcontroller contains two UART whose name are UART 0 and UART 01. These UARTs are provided the full mode control handshake interface during transmitting or receiving the data lines. These are used 16 Byte data rate during transmitting or receiving the data. For covering wide range of baud rate they also contain the built in functional baud rate generator, therefore there is no need of any external crystal of specific value.

I2C Bus Serial I/O Controller: I2 C bus serial is bidirectional multi master bus. It can easily control two or more buses which are connected to it. The data which is transferred for master bus to slave bus is transferred through this bidirectional bus at baud rate up 400 k. Similarly the serial clock synchronization allows the device to communicate the data of different baud rate pass through only one serial bus. This clock synchronization could be used as handshake mechanism for resuming or suspending the data transfer.

SPI Serial I/O Control: This SPI serial I/O control supports the duplex data transfer, means this control supports the device for transferring the data whose range 4 kB to 16 kB from master bus to slave bus. This operation is called synchronous serial communication operation from master but to slave bus. This data is transmitted or received in 8 frames and each frame is contains 4 bits to 16 bits.

Timers: This LPC 2148 microcontroller has two timers or counters. These timers are 32 bit and are programmable with 32 bit pre scaler value as well as it also has one external event counter. Each timer has four 32 bit capture channels which take the snapshot of timer value during the transition of any input signal. With the help of this capture event the interruption could be also generate.

Watch Dog Timer: This LPC 2148 microcontroller also contains the watch dog timer whose main purposes is to reset the microcontroller with in specific amount of time during erroneous state. After this state it again turned on the microcenter with in specific amount of time limit.

Real Time Clock (RTC): In this LPC 2148 microcontroller, the RTC is designed to set the counters for the measuring the whole time when the controller is in operating mode or idle mode. It has designed to consume little power which make it suitable for battery powered systems where CPU is not continually in operating mode.

Crystal Oscillator: This LPC 2148 microcontroller contains the on chip integrated oscillator which operate with an external crystal whose range is in between 1 MHz to 25 MHz Its output frequency is called focs and controller clock frequency is called CCLK. These names are used for making rate equation. These frequencies would be same when the PLL is connected and in running position.LPC 2148 ARM7 Microcontroller crystal

PLL: This LPC 2148 microcontroller contains two phase locked loops whose names are PLL0 and PLL1.The input frequency whose range is in between 1 MHz to 25 MHz is accepted by this PLL. This frequency range could be extended from 10 MHz to 60 MHz by using the current controlled oscillator (CCO).

LPC 2148 Microcontroller Registers: This LPC 2148 microcontroller also consists of one program status register and 16 general purposes registers whose names are R0 to R15. These register has wide range such as 8,16 and 32 bits. Beside this, it also consists of one shadow register which is selected such as operation mode switch.

Interrupts: It has vectored interrupt controller. VIC can be configured sixteen configurable priorities. LPC2148 microcontroller has 9 level or edge triggered external interrupts.

Power saving modes: It has power saving modes also like idle mode and sleep mode.

Different Types of Memory Modules used in Embedded System

An embedded system uses different types of memory modules for a wide range of tasks such as storage of software code and instructions for hardware. These software codes and instructions are used to program the microcontroller.

Different Types of Memory

Types of Memory Modules

Different types of memory modules for any system depend on the nature of application of that system. The memory performance and capability requirements are small for low cost systems. Selection of a memory module is the most critical requirement in a designing a microcontroller based project.

The following general types of memory module can be used in an embedded system.

- Volatile Memory
- Non-Volatile Memory

Volatile Memory Module - RAM

Volatile memory devices are types of storage devices which hold their content till power is applied to them.

When power is switched off, these memories lose their content.

An example of volatile memory device is Random Access Memory (RAM)

Volatile Memory Module-RAM

The RAM memory chip, referred to as a main memory, is a storage location that allows information to be stored and accessed quickly from random location with memory module. The memory cell which can be accessed for information transfer to or from any desired random location is called a Random Access Memory.

A RAM memory is designed with a collection of storage cells. Each cell contains either BJT or MOSFET based on type of memory module. For example, 4*4 RAM memory can store 4 bit of information.

Every instruction of a row and column in this matrix is a memory cell. Each block labeled BC, represents the binary cells with its 3 inputs and 1 output. Each block consists of 12 binary cells.

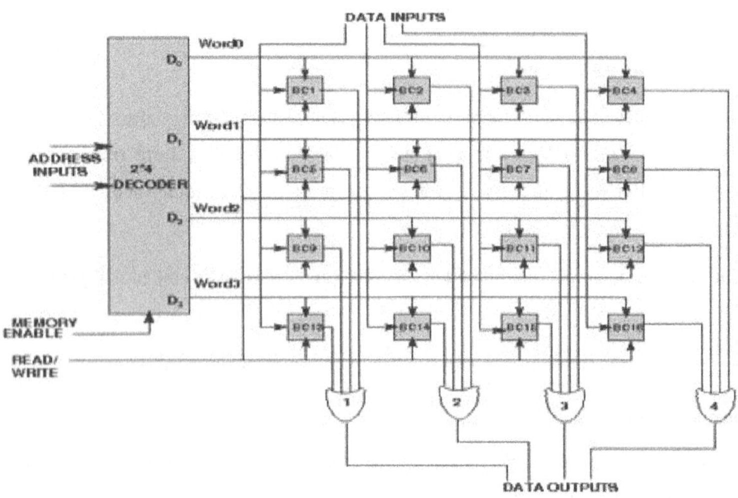

Internal Data Storage Circuit for RAM Memory

To each memory block, each word output from the decoder is the select input. The decoder is enabled with the memory enable input. When the memory enable pin is at logic low level, all outputs of the decoder are at logic low level and memory doesn't select any word. When the enable pin is at logic high level, the parallel output corresponding to the serial input is given as select input to each memory block.

Internal Data Storage Circuit for RAM Memory Chip

Once the word has been selected, the read and write pin for each block, determines the operation. If the read/write pin is at logic low level, the input is written onto the memory block. If the read/write pin is at logic high level, the output is read from each block.

Non- Volatile Memory-ROM Memory

Non-volatile memories are permanent storage types of memory chips which can get back stored information even when the power is switched off. An example of non-volatile memory device is Read Only Memory (ROM).

The ROM stands for Read Only Memory. ROM can only be used to read from, but cannot be written upon. These memory devices are non-volatile.

Non Volatile Memory-ROM Memory

A ROM family is designed with collection of storage cells. Each memory cell contains either bipolar or MOSFET transistor based on types of memory.

Types of RAM Chips Available

The RAM family includes two important memory devices which are:

Static Random Access Memory (SRAM)

The Static Random Access Memory module is a type of RAM that retains the data bits in its memory as long as power is being supplied. The SRAM does not need to be refreshed periodically. The static RAM provides faster access to the data and is more expensive than DRAM.

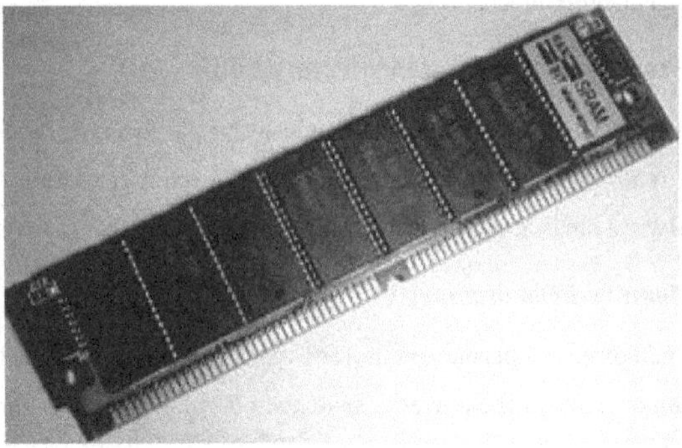

Static Random Access Memory (SRAM)

Each bit in an SRAM is stored in four transistors that form two cross coupled inverters. Two additional transistors – types serve to control the access to the storage cells during read and write operations. A typically SRAM uses six transistors to store each memory bit. These Storage Cells have two stable states which are used to denote '0' and '1'.

Advantages

- The external SRAM provide large storage capacities than on-chip memories.
- The SRAM devices can be even found in smaller and larger capacities.
- The SRAMs typically have very low latency and high performance.
- The SRAM memory can be designed and interfaced very easily compared to other memories

Applications

- The external SRAM is quite effective as a faster buffer for medium size block of data. You can use external SRAM to buffer data that does not fit in to on-chip memory and requires lower latency than what DRAM provides.
- If your system requires a block of memory larger than 10 MB, you can consider different types of memories such as SRAM.

Dynamic Random Access Memory

The Dynamic Random Access Memory is a type of RAM module that stores each bit of data within a separate capacitor. This is an efficient way to store the data in memory because it requires less physical space to store the data.

Dynamic Access Random Memory (DRAM)

A particular size of DRAM can hold more amounts of data than a SRAM chip with the same size. The capacitors in DRAM need to be constantly recharged to keep their charge. This is the reason why DRAM requires more power.

Each DRAM memory chip consists of a storage locations or memory cells. It is made up of capacitor and transistor which can hold either active or inactive state. Each DRAM cell is referred to as a bit.

When the DRAM cell holds a value at active state '1', the charge is at high state. When the DRAM cell holds a value at inactive state '0', the charge is below a certain level.

Advantages

- The storage capacity is very high
- It is a low cost device

Applications

- It is used for storing large block of data
- It is used in executing microprocessor code
- Applications where low latency memory access is required.

Types of ROM Memories

Different types of memory in the ROM family have four important memory devices which are:

Programmable Read Only Memory

The Programmable read only memory (PROM) can be modified only once by the user. The PROM is manufactured with series of fuses. The chip is programmed by the PROM programmer wherein some fuses are burnt. The open fuses are read as ones, while the burned fuses are read as zeros.

Programmable Read Only Memory

Erasable Programmable Read Only Memory

Erasable Programmable Read Only Memory

The erasable programmable read only memory is one of the special types of memory modules that can be programmed any number of times to correct the errors. It can retain its contents until exposed to ultraviolet light.

The ultraviolet light erases its contents making its possible to program the memory. To write and erase the EPROM memory chip, we need a special device called PROM programmer.

The EPROM is programmed by forcing electrical charge on a small piece of poly silicon metal known as floating gate, which is located in the memory cell. When charge is present in this gate the cell is programmed, i.e. memory contains '0'. When charge is not present in the gate, the cell is not programmed, i.e. memory contains '1'.

Electrical Erasable Programmable Read Only Memory

EEPROM is a user modified read only memory chip that can be erased and programmed for a number of times.

Electrically Erasable Programmable Read Only Memory

These memory devices are used in computers and other electronic devices to store small amount of data that must be saved when the power supply is removed. The content of EEPROM is erased by exposing it to an electrical charge.

The EEPROM data is stored and removed 1 byte of data at a time. The EEPROM does not need to be removed from the computer to be modified. The changing the content does not requires the additional equipment.

The modern EEPROM allows multi byte page operations and has limited life. The EEPROM can be designed 10 to 1000 write cycles. When the number of write operations is completed, the EEPROM stops working.

EEPROM is a storage device that can be implemented with fewer standards in cell design. The more common cell is composed of two transistors. The storage transistor has a floating gage similar to EPROM. The EEPROMs has two families which are serial EEPROM and parallel EEPROM. The parallel EEPROM is faster and cost effective then serial memory.

Flash Memory

The flash memory is the most widely used device for electronics and computer devices. The flash memory is among the special types of memory that can be erased and programmed with a block of data. The flash memory keeps its data even with no power at all. The flash memory is popular because it works fast and efficiently than EEPROM.

Flash Memory

The flash memory module is designed for about 100000 -10000000 write cycles. The main constraint with the flash memory is number of times data can be written to it. The data can be read from flash memory as many times as desired, but after a certain number of write operations, it will stop working.

On-Chip Memory

The On-Chip memory is referred to any memory module like RAM, ROM or other memories but that physically exits on the microcontroller itself. Different microcontrollers -types like 8051 microcontroller has limited On-Chip ROM memory. However it has a capability of expanding to a maximum of 64KB of external ROM memory and 64KB external RAM memory.

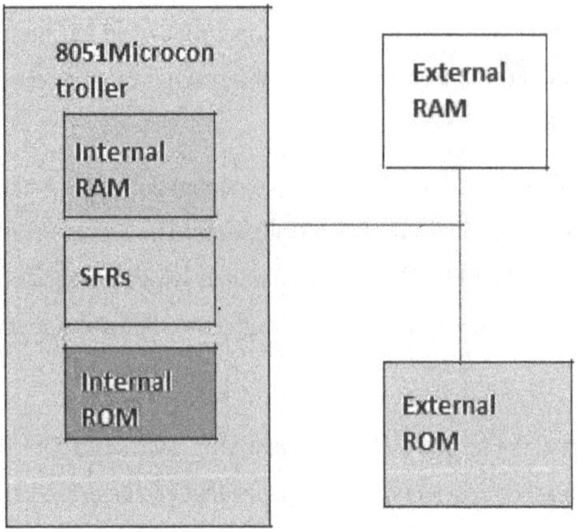

On-Chip Memory

The /EA pin is used to control the external and internal memories of the microcontroller. If /EA pin is connected to 5V, then data is fetched to or from the internal memory of the microcontroller. When /EA pin is connected to the ground, the data is fetched to or from the external memories.

I hope by now you must be having a clear understanding about different types of memory. Here is a basic question for you- To design any embedded system, which type of ROM and RAM is usually used and why?

Give your answers in the comment section below.

Photo Credit:

Different types of Memory Modules by klbict

Volatile Memory module-RAM by wikimedia

Non Volatile memory module-ROM memory by yuvayana

Static Random Access Memory by 2.bp.blogspot

Dynamic Random Access Memory by directindustry

Programmable Read Only Memory by touque

Erasable Programmable Read Only Memory by qcwo

Electrical Erasable Programmable Read Only Memory by amitbhawani

Flash Memory by Encrypted-tbn1.gstatic

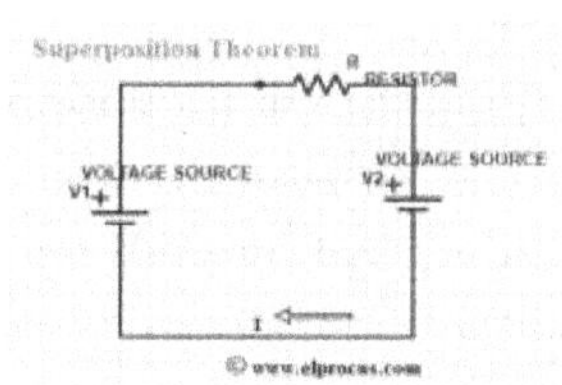

Superposition Theorem: Example Problems, Limitations and Applications

ARM7 Based (LPC2148) Microcontroller Pin Configuration

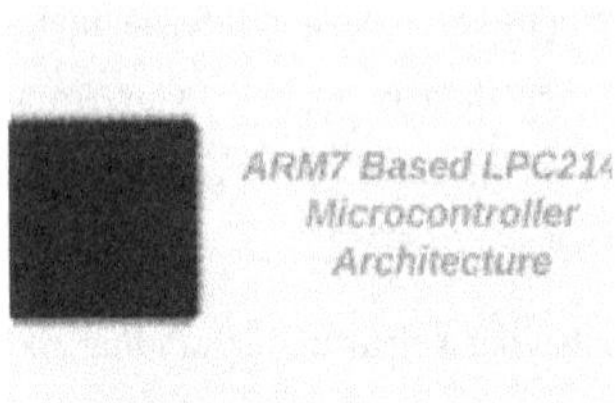

Introduction to ARM7 Based LPC2148 Microcontroller Architecture

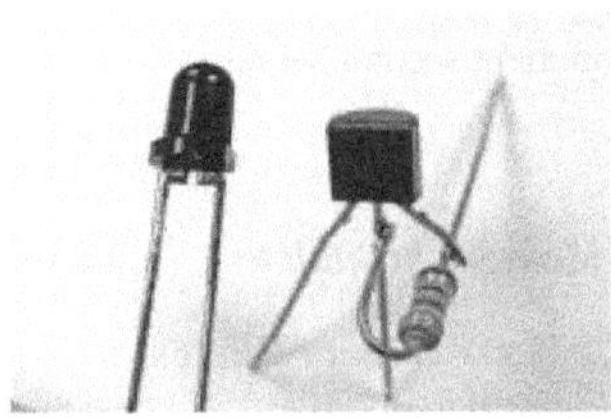

Phototransistor Basics, Circuit Diagram, Advantages & Applications

Processors

Amazing processors utilized in embedded systems are microprocessor, (DSP) virtual sign processor, microcontroller, RISC processor, ASIP processor, arm processor and ASSP processor.

Characteristics of Embedded System

- Using the embedded gadget definition it's far possible to recognize the numerous basic traits one. Normally they're:
- Embedded systems are designed for a specific challenge. Even though they use laptop strategies, they cannot be used as a widespread reason computer the use of a spread of different programs for one of a kind project. On this manner, their function can be focused on what they need to do, and they can consequently be made inexpensive and greater correctly.
- The software program program for embedded systems is usually called firmware. In preference to being saved on a disc, where many applications can be stored, the single programmed for an embedded gadget is usually saved on the chip and its miles called firmware.
- Commonly, an embedded device executes a particular operation and does the similar always. As an example: a pager is continuously functioning as a pager.

- All of the computing structures have boundaries on layout metrics, but the ones can be in particular tight. Design calculation is a measure of executive functions like length, strength, price and also performance.
- It should carry out rapid sufficient and eat much less strength to increase battery existence.
- Several embedded systems have to continuously react to modifications inside the system and also calculate precise outcomes in actual time without any put-off. For instance, an automobile cruise controller; it constantly shows and responds to hurry & brake sensors. It should calculate acceleration/de-accelerations often in a restrained time; a behind schedule computation can outcome in letdown to manipulate the automobile.
- It has to be based totally on a microcontroller or microprocessor primarily based.
- An embedded system is built in with hardware and software program where the hardware is used for safety and performance and software is used for more flexibility and capabilities.

4.4. Quality Attributes of Embedded System

These are the attributes that together form the deciding factor about the quality of an embedded system.

There are two types of quality attributes are:-

Operational Quality Attributes

These are attributes related to operation or functioning of an embedded system. The way an embedded system operates affects its overall quality.

Notable quality attributes include:

- accessibility
- accountability
- accuracy
- adaptability
- administrability
- affordability
- agility [Toll] (see Common Subsets below)
- auditability
- autonomy [Erl]
- availability

- compatibility
- composability [Erl]
- configurability
- correctness
- credibility
- customizability
- debugability
- degradability
- determinability
- demonstrability
- dependability
- deployability
- discoverability [Erl]
- distributability
- durability
- effectiveness
- efficiency
- evolvability
- extensibility
- failure transparency
- fault-tolerance
- fidelity
- flexibility
- inspectability
- installability
- integrity
- interchangeability
- interoperability [Erl]
- learnability
- maintainability
- manageability
- mobility
- modifiability
- modularity

- operability
- orthogonality
- portability
- precision
- predictability
- process capabilities
- producibility
- provability
- recoverability
- relevance
- reliability
- repeatability
- reproducibility
- resilience
- responsiveness
- reusability [Erl]
- robustness
- safety
- scalability
- seamlessness
- self-sustainability
- serviceability (a.k.a. supportability)
- securability
- simplicity
- stability
- standards compliance
- survivability
- sustainability
- tailorability
- testability
- timeliness
- traceability
- transparency
- ubiquity

- understandability
- upgradability
- vulnerability
- usability

Many of these quality attributes can also be applied to data quality.

Common Subsets

- Together, reliability, availability, serviceability, usability and install ability, are referred to as RASUI.
- Functionality, usability, reliability, performance and supportability are together referred to as FURPS in relation to software requirements.
- Agility in working software is an aggregation of seven architecturally sensitive attributes: debug ability, extensibility, portability, scalability, securability, testability and understandability.
- For databases reliability, availability, scalability and recoverability (RASR), is an important concept.
- Atomicity, consistency, isolation (sometimes integrity), durability (ACID) is a transaction metric.
- When dealing with safety-critical systems, the acronym reliability, availability, maintainability and safety (RAMS) is frequently used.
- Dependability is an aggregate of availability, reliability, safety, integrity and maintainability.
    - Integrity depends on security and survivability.
    - Security is a composite of confidentiality, integrity and availability. Security and dependability are often treated together.

Non-Operational Quality Attributes

These are attributes **not** related to operation or functioning of an embedded system. The way an embedded system operates affects its overall quality.

These are the attributes that are associated with the embedded system before it can be put in operation.

Operational Attributes

Response

Response is a measure of quickness of the system.

It gives you an idea about how fast your system is tracking the input variables.

Most of the embedded system demand fast response which should be real-time.

Throughput

Throughput deals with the efficiency of system.

It can be defined as rate of production or process of a defined process over a stated period of time.

In case of card reader like the ones used in buses, throughput means how much transaction the reader can perform in a minute or hour or day.

Reliability

Reliability is a measure of how much percentage you rely upon the proper functioning of the system. Mean Time between failures and Mean Time To Repair are terms used in defining system reliability.

Mean Time between failures can be defined as the average time the system is functioning before a failure occurs.

Mean time to repair can be defined as the average time the system has spent in repairs.

Maintainability

Maintainability deals with support and maintenance to the end user or a client in case of technical issues and product failures or on the basis of a routine system checkup

It can be classified into two types:-

Scheduled or Periodic Maintenance

This is the maintenance that is required regularly after a periodic time interval.

Example

Periodic Cleaning of Air Conditioners.

Refilling of printer cartridges.

Maintenance to Unexpected Failure

This involves the maintenance due to a sudden breakdown in the functioning of the system.

Example

Air conditioner not powering on Printer not taking paper in spite of a full paper stack

Security

- Confidentiality, Integrity and Availability are three corner stones of information security.

Confidentiality deals with protection data from unauthorized disclosure.

Integrity gives protection from unauthorized modification.

Availability gives protection from unauthorized user

Certain Embedded systems have to make sure they conform to the security measures.

Ex. An Electronic Safety Deposit Locker can be used only with a pin number like a password.

Safety

Safety deals with the possible damage that can happen to the operating person and environment due to the breakdown of an embedded system or due to the emission of hazardous materials from the embedded products.

A safety analysis is a must in product engineering to evaluate the anticipated damage and determine the best course of action to bring down the consequence of damages to an acceptable level.

Non Operational Attributes

Testability and Debug-ability

- It deals with how easily one can test his/her design, application and by which mean he/she can test it.
- In hardware testing the peripherals and total hardware function in designed manner
- Firmware testing is functioning in expected way
- Debug-ability is means of debugging the product as such for figuring out the probable sources that create unexpected behavior in the total system

Evolvability

- For embedded system, the qualitative attribute "Evolvability" refer to ease with which the embedded product can be modified to take advantage of new firmware or hardware technology.

Portability

- Portability is measured of "system Independence".

- An embedded product can be called portable if it is capable of performing its operation as it is intended to do in various environments irrespective of different processor and or controller and embedded operating systems.

Time to Prototype and Market

Time to Market is the time elapsed between the conceptualization of a product and time at which the product is ready for selling or use

Product prototyping help in reducing time to market.

Prototyping is an informal kind of rapid product development in which important feature of the under consider are develop.

In order to shorten the time to prototype, make use of all possible option like use of reuse, off the self component etc.

Per Unit and Total Cost

Cost is an important factor which needs to be carefully monitored. Proper market study and cost benefit analysis should be carried out before taking decision on the per unit cost of the embedded product.

When the product is introduced in the market, for the initial period the sales and revenue will be low

There won't be much competition when the product sales and revenue increase.

During the maturing phase, the growth will be steady and revenue reaches highest point and at retirement time there will be a drop in sales volume.

1. IT-51061 Introduction to EMBEDDED SYSTEM (2nd Edition) SHIBU K V Dr Moe Moe Myint Department of Computer Engineering & Information Technology Mandalay Technological University www.slideshare.net/MoeMoeMyint moemoemyint@moe myanmar. mlmoe2myint.mdy@gmail.com drmoemoemyint.blogspot.com
2. Agenda 3.1 Characteristics of Embedded Systems 3.2 Quality Attributes of Embedded Systems 2 Mandalay Technological University Department of Computer Engineering and Information Technology Lecture Slides for Textbook Introduction to Embedded Systems, Moe Moe Myint, 2017-2018
3. Understand the Product Life Cycle (PLC) 3 Mandalay Technological University Department of Computer Engineering and Information Technology Lecture Slides for Textbook Introduction to Embedded Systems, Moe Moe Myint, 2017-2018♣ Learn the

important quality attributes of the embedded system that needs to be addressed for the non-operational mode (offline mode) of the system. This includes Testability, Debug-ability, Evolvability, Portability, Time to prototype and market, Per unit cost and revenue, etc. ♣ Learn the important quality attributes of the embedded system that needs to be addressed for the operational mode (online mode) of the system. This includes Response, Throughput, Reliability, Maintainability, Security, Safety, etc. ♣ Learn the non-functional requirements that needs to be addressed in the design of an embedded system ♣ Learn the characteristics describing an embedded system ♣Learning Objectives

4. This chapter gives a brief introduction on the characteristics of an embedded system and the attributes that are associated with its quality. 4 Mandalay Technological University Department of Computer Engineering and Information Technology Lecture Slides for Textbook Introduction to Embedded Systems, Moe Moe Myint, 2017-2018♣ The characteristics of embedded system are different from those of a general purpose computer and so are its Quality metrics. ♣Introduction.
5. Some of the important characteristics of an embedded system are: 1. Application and domain specific 2. Reactive and Real Time 3. Operates in harsh environments 4. Distributed 5. Small size and weight 6. Power concerns 5 Mandalay Technological University Department of Computer Engineering and Information Technology Lecture Slides for Textbook Introduction to Embedded Systems, Moe Moe Myint, 2017-2018♣ Unlike general purpose computing systems, embedded systems possess certain specific characteristics and these characteristics are unique to each embedded system. ♣3.1 Characteristics of an Embedded System
6. Certain embedded systems are specific to a domain: ex. A hearing aid is an application that belongs to the domain of signal processing and telecom with another control unit designed to serve another domain like consumer electronics. 6 Mandalay Technological University Department of Computer Engineering and Information Technology Lecture Slides for Textbook Introduction to Embedded Systems, Moe Moe Myint, 2017-2018♣ Because the embedded control units of microwave oven and air conditioner are specifically designed to perform certain specific tasks. ♣ Ex. A washing machine can only wash, it cannot cook.. ♣ Ex. Air conditioner's embedded control unit, it cannot replace microwave oven... ♣ It will not do any other task. ♣ An embedded system is designed for a specific purpose only. ♣1. Application and Domain Specific

7. An embedded system uses Sensors to take inputs and has actuators to bring out the required functionality. 7 Mandalay Technological University Department of Computer Engineering and Information Technology Lecture Slides for Textbook Introduction to Embedded Systems, Moe Moe Myint, 2017-2018♣ Ex. An air conditioner adjusts its mechanical parts as soon as it gets a signal from its sensors to increase or decrease the temperature when the user operates it using a remote control. ♣ Ex. Flight control systems, Antilock Brake Systems (ABS), etc. are examples of Real Time systems ♣ Certain embedded systems are designed to react to the events that occur in the nearby environment. These events also occur real-time. ♣2. Reactive and Real Time
8. Certain embedded systems ar♣3. Operation in Harsh Environment These embedded systems have to be capable of sustaining the environmental conditions it is designed to operate in. 8 Mandalay Technological University Department of Computer Engineering and Information Technology Lecture Slides for Textbook Introduction to Embedded Systems, Moe Moe Myint, 2017-2018♣e designed to operate in harsh environments like a dusty one or a high temperature zone or an area subject to vibrations and shock or very high temperature of the deserts or very low temperature of the mountains or extreme rains.
9. This can visualize these as independent embedded systems. But they work together to achieve a common goal. 9 Mandalay Technological University Department of Computer Engineering and Information Technology Lecture Slides for Textbook Introduction to Embedded Systems, Moe Moe Myint, 2017-2018♣ Ex. Automatic Teller Machine (ATM) contains a card reader embedded unit, responsible for reading and validating the user's ATM card, transaction unit for performing transactions, a currency counter for dispatching/vending currency to the authorized person and a printer unit for printing the transaction details. ♣ Ex. An automatic vending machine is a typical example for this. The vending machine contains a card reader (for pre-paid vending systems), a vending unit, etc. Each of them are independent embedded units but they work together to perform the overall vending function. ♣ These components are independent of each other but have to work together for the larger system to function properly. ♣ The term distributed means that embedded systems may be a part of a larger system. ♣4. Distributed
10. Ex. Currently available cell phones. The cell phones that have the maximum features are popular but also their size and weight is an important characteristic. 10 Mandalay Technological University Department of Computer Engineering and Information

Technology Lecture Slides for Textbook Introduction to Embedded Systems, Moe Moe Myint, 2017-2018♣ An embedded system that is compact in size and has light weight will be desirable or more popular than one that is bulky and heavy. ♣5. Small Size and Weight

11. The more the power consumption the less is the battery life. 11 Mandalay Technological University Department of Computer Engineering and Information Technology Lecture Slides for Textbook Introduction to Embedded Systems, Moe Moe Myint, 2017-2018♣ Also power management is a critical constraint in battery operated application. ♣ Select the design according to the low power components like low dropout regulators, and controllers/processors with power saving modes. ♣ Ex. The production of high amount of heat demands cooling requirements like cooling fans which in turn occupies additional space and make the system bulky. Nowadays ultra low power components are available in the market. ♣ If more heat is dissipated then additional units like heat sinks or cooling fans need to be added to the circuit. ♣ It is desirable that the power utilization and heat dissipation of any embedded system be low. ♣6. Power Concerns
12. The various quality attributes that needs to be addressed in any embedded system development are broadly classified into two, namely i. Operational Quality Attributes ii. Non-Operational Quality Attributes 12 Mandalay Technological University Department of Computer Engineering and Information Technology Lecture Slides for Textbook Introduction to Embedded Systems, Moe Moe Myint, 2017-2018♣ If the quality attributes are more concrete and measurable, it will give a positive impact on the system development process and the end product. ♣ Quality attributes are the non-functional requirements that need to be documented properly in any system design. ♣3.2 Quality Attributes of Embedded Systems
13. The operational quality attributes represent the relevant quality attributes related to the embedded system when it is in the operational mode or 'online' mode. The important quality attributes coming under this category are listed below: i. Response ii. Throughput iii. Reliability iv. Maintainability v. Security vi. Safety 13 Mandalay Technological University Department of Computer Engineering and Information Technology Lecture Slides for Textbook Introduction to Embedded Systems, Moe Moe Myint, 2017-2018♣1. Operational Quality Attributes

14. Reading Assignment 14 Mandalay Technological University Department of Computer Engineering and Information Technology Lecture Slides for Textbook Introduction to Embedded Systems, Moe Moe Myint, 2017-2018
15. It is♣ Any response delay in the system will create potential damages to the safety of the flight as well as the passengers. ♣ Ex. An embedded system deployed in flight control application should respond in a Real Time manner. ♣ Most of the embedded system demand fast response which should be real-time. ♣ It gives you an idea about how fast your system is tracking the input variables. ♣ Response is a measure of quickness of the system. ♣i. Response For example, the response time requirement for an electronic toy is not at all time-critical. 15 Mandalay Technological University Department of Computer Engineering and Information Technology Lecture Slides for Textbook Introduction to Embedded Systems, Moe Moe Myint, 2017-2018♣not necessary that all embedded systems should be Real Time in response.
16. Benchmark can be a set of performance criteria that a product is expected to meet or a standard product that can be used for comparing other products of the same product line. 16 Mandalay Technological University Department of Computer Engineering and Information Technology Lecture Slides for Textbook Introduction to Embedded Systems, Moe Moe Myint, 2017-2018♣ Throughput is generally measured in terms of 'Benchmark'. A 'Benchmark' is a reference point by which something can be measured. ♣ In case of card reader like the ones used in buses, throughput means how much transactions the Reader can perform in a minute or hour or day. ♣ The rates can be expressed in terms of units of products, batches produced, or any other meaningful measurements. ♣ It can be defined as rate of production or process of a defined process over a stated period of time. ♣ Throughput deals with the efficiency of system. ♣ii. Throughput
17. For an embedded system with critical application need, it should be of the order of minutes. 17 Mandalay Technological University Department of Computer Engineering and Information Technology Lecture Slides for Textbook Introduction to Embedded Systems, Moe Moe Myint, 2017-2018♣ MTTR specifies how long the system is allowed to be out of order following a failure. ♣ MTBF gives the frequency of failures in hours/weeks/months. ♣ Mean Time Between Failures (MTBF) and Mean Time To Repair (MTTR) are the terms used in defining system reliability. ♣ Reliability is a measure of how much percentage you rely upon the proper functioning of the system or what is the % susceptibility of the system to failure. ♣iii. Reliability

18. Maintainability can be classified into two types: 1. Scheduled or Periodic Maintenance (Preventive Maintenance) An inkjet printer uses ink cartridges, which are consumable components and as per the printer manufacturer the end use should replace the cartridge after each 'n' number of printouts to get quality prints. 2. Maintenance to Unexpected Failures (Corrective Maintenance) If the paper feeding part of the printer fails the printer fails to print and it requires immediate repairs to rectify this problem. Hence it is obvious that maintainability is simply an indication of the availability of the product for use. In any embedded system design, the ideal value for availability is expressed as $\boldsymbol{Ai} = \boldsymbol{MTBF/}\ (\boldsymbol{MTBF} + \boldsymbol{MTTR})$ Where Ai=Availability in the ideal condition, MTBF=Mean Time Between Failures, and MTTR= Mean Time To Repair 18 Mandalay Technological University Department of Computer Engineering and Information Technology Lecture Slides for Textbook Introduction to Embedded Systems, Moe Moe Myint, 2017-2018♣ Reliability and maintainability are considered as two complementary disciplines. A more reliable system means a system with less corrective maintainability requirements and vice versa. ♣ Maintainability deals with support and maintenance to the end user or client in case of technical issues and product failures or on the basis of a routine system checkup. ♣iv. Maintainability
19. Ex. An electronic safety Deposit Locker can be used only with a pin number like a password. 19 Mandalay Technological University Department of Computer Engineering and Information Technology Lecture Slides for Textbook Introduction to Embedded Systems, Moe Moe Myint, 2017-2018♣ Certain embedded systems have to make sure they conform to the security measures. ♣ 'Availability' deals with protection of data and application from unauthorized users. ♣ 'Integrity' deals with the protection of data and application from unauthorized modification. ♣ 'Confidentially' deals with the protection of data and application from unauthorized disclosure. ♣ 'Confidentially', 'Integrity', and 'Availability' are three major measures of information security. ♣v. Security
20. Safety analysis is a must in product engineering to evaluate the anticipated damages and determine the best course of action to bring down the consequences of the damages to an acceptable level. 20 Mandalay Technological University Department of Computer Engineering and Information Technology Lecture Slides for Textbook Introduction to Embedded Systems, Moe Moe Myint, 2017-2018♣ The breakdown of an embedded system may occur due to a hardware failure or a firmware failure. ♣ Safety deals with the possible damages that can happen to the operators, public and the

environment due to the breakdown of an embedded system or due to the emission of radioactive or hazardous materials from the embedded products. ♣vi. Safety

21. The quality attributes that needs to be addressed for the product 'not' on the basic of operational aspects are grouped under this category. The important quality attributes coming under this category are listed below: i. Testability♣2. Non Operational Attributes & Debug-ability ii. Evolvability iii. Portability iv. Time to prototype and market v. Per unit and total cost 21 Mandalay Technological University Department of Computer Engineering and Information Technology Lecture Slides for Textbook Introduction to Embedded Systems, Moe Moe Myint, 2017-2018
22. i. Testability & Hardware debugging is used for figuring out the issues created by hardware problems whereas firmware debugging is employed to figure out the probable errors that appear as a result of flaws in the firmware. 22 Mandalay Technological University Department of Computer Engineering and Information Technology Lecture Slides for Textbook Introduction to Embedded Systems, Moe Moe Myint, 2017-2018♣ Debug-ability has two aspects in the embedded system development context, namely, hardware level debugging and firmware level debugging. ♣ Debug-ability is a means of debugging the product as such for figuring out the probable sources that create unexpected behavior in the total system. ♣ For an embedded product, testability is applicable to both the embedded hardware and firmware. ♣ Testability deals with how easily one can test his/her design, application and by which means he/she can test it. ♣Debug-ability
23. For an embedded system, the quality attribute 'Evolvability' refers to the ease with which the embedded product (including firmware and hardware) can be modified to take advantage of new firmware or hardware technologies. 23 Mandalay Technological University Department of Computer Engineering and Information Technology Lecture Slides for Textbook Introduction to Embedded Systems, Moe Moe Myint, 2017-2018♣ Evolvability is referred as the non-heritable variation. ♣ Evolvability is a term which is closely related to Biology. ♣ii. Evolvability
24. A standard embedded product should always be flexible and portable. 24 Mandalay Technological University Department of Computer Engineering and Information Technology Lecture Slides for Textbook Introduction to Embedded Systems, Moe Moe Myint, 2017-2018♣ An embedded product can be called portable if it is capable of functioning in various environments, target processors/controllers and embedded operating systems. ♣ Portability is a measure of 'system independence'. ♣iii. Portability

25. Product prototyping helps a lot in reducing time-to-market. 25 Mandalay Technological University Department of Computer Engineering and Information Technology Lecture Slides for Textbook Introduction to Embedded Systems, Moe Moe Myint, 2017-2018♣ The commercial embedded product market is highly competitive and time to market the product is a critical factor in the success of a commercial embedded product. ♣ Time-to-market is the time elapsed between the conceptualization of a product and the time at which the product is ready for selling (for commercial product) or use (for non-commercial products). ♣iv. Time-to-Prototype and Market
26. During the maturing phase, the growth will be steady and revenue reaches highest point and at retirement time there will be a drop in sales volume. 26 Mandalay Technological University Department of Computer Engineering and Information Technology Lecture Slides for Textbook Introduction to Embedded Systems, Moe Moe Myint, 2017-2018♣ There won't be much competition when the product sales and revenue increase. ♣ When the product is introduced in the market, for the initial period the sales and revenue will be low. ♣ Proper market study and cost benefit analysis should be carried out before taking decision on the per unit cost of the embedded product. ♣ Cost is a highly sensitive factor for commercial products. ♣ Cost is a factor which is closely monitored by both end user (those who buy the product) and product manufacturer (those who build the product). ♣v. Per Unit Cost and Revenue
27. Cont'd27 Mandalay Technological University Department of Computer Engineering and Information Technology Lecture Slides for Textbook Introduction to Embedded Systems, Moe Moe Myint, 2017-2018 Product life cycle (PLC) curve.
28. Objective Questions28 Mandalay Technological University Department of Computer Engineering and Information Technology 1. Embedded systems are application and domain specific. State True or False (a) True (b) False 2. Which of the following is true about Embedded Systems? (a) Reactive and Real Time (b) Distributed (c) Operates in harsh environment (d) All of these (e) None of these 3. Which of the following is a distributed embedded system? (a) Cell phone (b) Notebook Computer (c) SCADA system (d) All of these (e) None of these 4. Quality attributes of an embedded system are (a) Functional requirements (b) Non-functional requirements (c) Both (d) None of these 5. Response is a measure of (a) Quickness of the system (b) How fast the system tracks changes in Input (c) Both (d) None of these Lecture Slides for Textbook Introduction to Embedded Systems, Moe Moe Myint, 2017-2018

29. Cont'd29 Mandalay Technological University Department of Computer Engineering and Information Technology 6. Throughput of an embedded system is a measure of (a) The efficiency of the system (b) The output over a stated period of time (c) Both (d) None of these 7. Benchmark is (a) A reference point (b) A set of performance criteria (c) (a) or (b) (d) None of these 8. Mean Time Between Failures (MTBF) and Mean Time To Repair (MTTR) defines the reliability of an embedded system. State True or False (a) True (b) False 9. MTBF gives the frequency of failures of an embedded system. State True or False (a) True (b) False 10. Which of the following is true about the quality attribute 'maintainability'? (a) The corrective maintainability requirement for a highly reliable embedded system is very less (b) Availability of an embedded system is directly related to the maintainability of the system (c) Both of these (d) None of these Lecture Slides for Textbook Introduction to Embedded Systems, Moe Moe Myint, 2017-2018
30. Cont'd30 Mandalay Technological University Department of Computer Engineering and Information Technology 11. The Mean Time Between Failure (MTBF) for an embedded product is very high. This means: (a) The product is highly reliable (b) The availability of the product is very high (c) The preventive maintenance requirement for the product is very less (d) All of these (e) None of these 12. The Mean Time Between Failure (MTBF) of an embedded product is 4 months and the Mean Time To Repair (MTTR) of the product is 2 weeks. What is the availability of the product? (a) 100% (b) 50% (c) 89% (d) 10% 13. Which of the following are the three measures of information security in embedded systems? (a) Confidentiality, secrecy, integrity (b) Confidentiality, integrity, availability (c) Confidentiality, transparency, availability (d) Integrity, transparency, availability Lecture Slides for Textbook Introduction to Embedded Systems, Moe Moe Myint, 2017-2018
31. Review Questions31 Mandalay Technological University Department of Computer Engineering and Information Technology 1. Explain the different characteristics of embedded systems in detail. Lecture Slides for Textbook Introduction to Embedded Systems, Moe Moe Myint, 2017-2018
32. This PPT is only for fair academic use. 32 Mandalay Technological University Department of Computer Engineering and Information Technology♣ Only Original Owner has full rights reserved for copied images. ♣

UNIT 5

TASK COMMUNICATION

5.1. Shared Memory

In computer programming, shared memory is a method by which program processes can exchange data more quickly than by reading and writing using the regular operating system services. For example, a client process may have data to pass to a server process that the server process is to modify and return to the client. Ordinarily, this would require the client writing to an output file (using the buffers of the operating system) and the server then reading that file as input from the buffers to its own work space. Using a designated area of shared memory, the data can be made directly accessible to both processes without having to use the system services. To put the data in shared memory, the client gets access to shared memory after checking a semaphore value, writes the data, and then resets the semaphore to signal to the server (which periodically checks shared memory for possible input) that data is waiting. In turn, the server process writes data back to the shared memory area, using the semaphore to indicate that data is ready to be read.

Other forms of interprocess communication (IPC) include message queueing, semaphores, and sockets.

What is Shared Memory?

In the discussion of the **fork()** system call, we mentioned that a parent and its children have separate address spaces.

While this would provide a more secured way of executing parent and children processes (because they will not interfere each other), they shared nothing and have no way to communicate with each other.

A ***shared memory*** is an extra piece of memory that is *attached* to some address spaces for their owners to use. As a result, all of these processes share the same memory segment and have access to it. Consequently, race conditions may occur if memory accesses are not handled properly. The following figure shows two processes and their address spaces. The yellow rectangle is a shared memory attached to both address spaces and both process 1 and process 2 can have access to this shared memory as if the shared memory is part of its own address space. In some sense, the original address spaces is "extended" by attaching this shared memory.

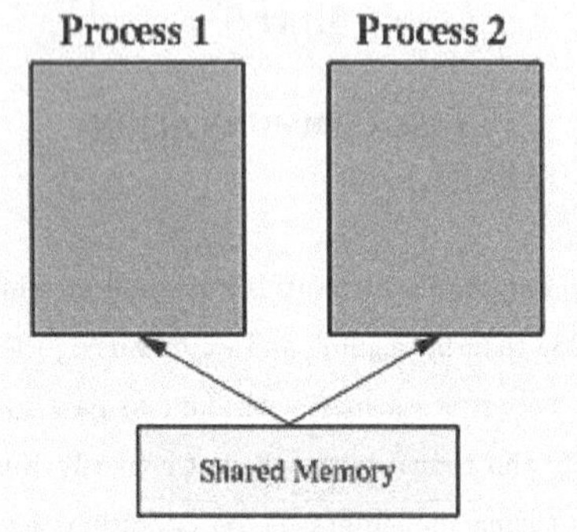

Shared memory is a feature supported by UNIX System V, including Linux, SunOS and Solaris. One process must explicitly ask for an area, using a ***key***, to be shared by other processes. This process will be called the *server*. All other processes, the *clients*, that know the shared area can access it. However, there is no protection to a shared memory and any process that knows it can access it freely. To protect a shared memory from being accessed at the same time by several processes, a synchronization protocol must be setup.

A shared memory segment is identified by a unique integer, the ***shared memory ID***. The shared memory itself is described by a structure of type **shmid_ds** in header file **sys/shm.h.** To use this file, files**sys/types.h** and **sys/ipc.h** must be included. Therefore, your program should start with the following lines:

```
#include <sys/types.h>
#include <sys/ipc.h>
#include <sys/shm.h>
```

A general scheme of using shared memory is the following:

- For a server, it should be started before any client. The server should perform the following tasks:
    1. Ask for a shared memory with a memory key and memorize the returned shared memory ID. This is performed by system call **shmget()**.
    2. Attach this shared memory to the server's address space with system call **shmat()**.
    3. Initialize the shared memory, if necessary.
    4. Do something and wait for all clients' completion.
    5. Detach the shared memory with system call **shmdt()**.
    6. Remove the shared memory with system call **shmctl()**.

- For the client part, the procedure is almost the same:
    1. Ask for a shared memory with the same memory key and memorize the returned shared memory ID.
    2. Attach this shared memory to the client's address space.
    3. Use the memory.
    4. Detach all shared memory segments, if necessary.
    5. Exit.

On the next few pages, we shall describe these system calls and their uses.

Message Passing

Message passing is a type of communication between processes or objects in computer science. In this model, processes or objects can send and receive messages (signals, functions, complex data structures, or data packets) to other processes or objects.

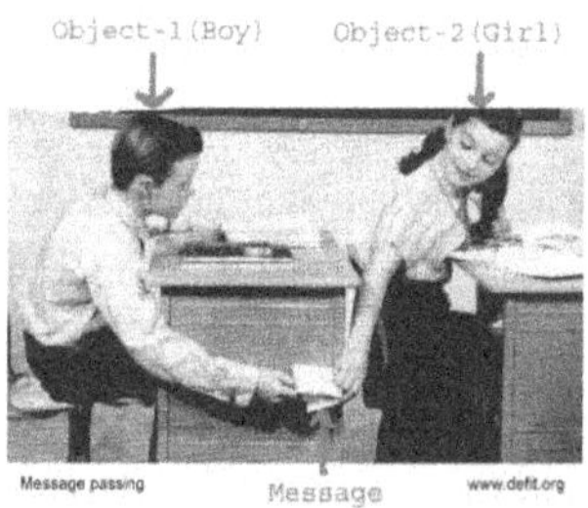

Message Passing Definition

Message passing is a form of communication between objects, processes or other resources used in object-oriented programming, inter-process communication and parallel computing.

Message passing can be synchronous or asynchronous. Synchronous message passing systems require the sender and receiver to wait for each other while transferring the message. In asynchronous communication the sender and receiver do not wait for each other and can carry on their own computations while transfer of messages is being done. The concept of message passing makes it easier to build systems that model or simulate real-world problems.

Inter Process Communication

A process can be of two type:

- Independent process.
- Co-operating process.

An independent process is not affected by the execution of other processes while a co-operating process can be affected by other executing processes. Though one can think that those processes, which are running independently, will execute very efficiently but in practical, there are many situations when co-operative nature can be utilised for increasing computational speed, convenience and modularity. Inter process communication (IPC) is a mechanism which allows processes to communicate each other and synchronize their actions. The communication between these processes can be seen as a method of co-operation between them. Processes can communicate with each other using these two ways:

1. Shared Memory
2. Message passing

An operating system can implement both method of communication. First, we will discuss the shared memory method of communication and then message passing. Communication between processes using shared memory requires processes to share some variable and it completely depends on how programmer will implement it. One way of communication using shared memory can be imagined like this: Suppose process1 and process2 are executing simultaneously and they share some resources or use some information from other process, process1 generate information about certain computations or resources being used and keeps it as a record in shared memory. When process2 need to use the shared information, it will check in the record stored in shared memory and take note of the information generated by process1 and act accordingly. Processes can use shared memory for extracting information as a record from other process as well as for delivering any specific information to other process.

Let's discuss an example of communication between processes using shared memory method.

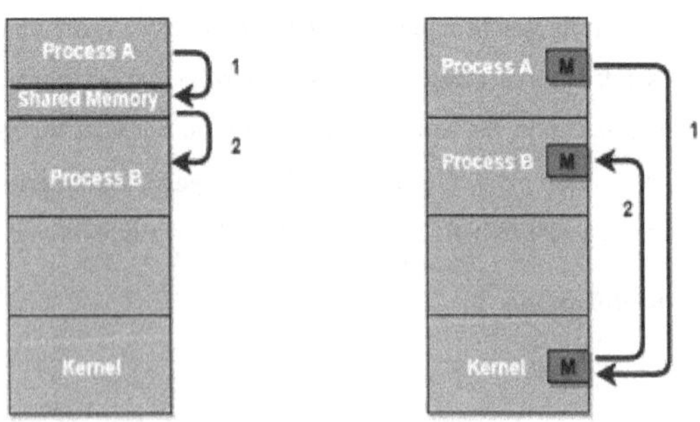

Figure 5.1: Shared Memory and Message Passing

i) Shared Memory Method

Ex: Producer-Consumer Problem

There are two processes: Producer and Consumer. Producer produces some item and Consumer consumes that item. The two processes shares a common space or memory location known as buffer where the item produced by Producer is stored and from where the Consumer consumes the item if needed. There are two version of this problem: first one is known as unbounded buffer problem in which Producer can keep on producing items and there is no limit on size of buffer, the second one is known as bounded buffer problem in which producer can produce up to a certain amount of item and after that it starts waiting for consumer to consume it. We will discuss the bounded buffer problem. First, the Producer and the Consumer will share some common memory, then producer will start producing items. If the total produced item is equal to the size of buffer, producer will wait to get it consumed by the Consumer. Similarly, the consumer first check for the availability of the item and if no item is available, Consumer will wait for producer to produce it. If there are items available, consumer will consume it. The pseudo code are given below:

Shared Data between the two Processes

```
#define buff_max 25
#define mod %
struct item{
// diffrent member of the produced data
// or consumed data
---------
}
// An array is needed for holding the items.
// This is the shared place which will be
// access by both process
// item shared_buff [ buff_max ];
// Two variables which will keep track of
// the indexes of the items produced by producer
// and consumer The free index points to
// the next free index. The full index points to
// the first full index.
int free_index = 0;
```

```
int full_index = 0;
```

Producer Process Code

```
item next Produced;
while(1){
// check if there is no space
// for production.
// if so keep waiting.
while((free_index+1) mod buff_max == full_index);
shared_buff[free_index] = nextProduced;
free_index = (free_index + 1) mod buff_max;
}
```

Consumer Process Code

```
item next Consumed;
while(1){
// check if there is an available
// item  for consumption.
// if not keep on waiting for
// get them produced.
while((free_index == full_index);
nextConsumed = shared_buff[full_index];
full_index = (full_index + 1) mod buff_max;
}
```

In the above code, The producer will start producing again when the (free_index+1) mod buff max will be free because if it it not free, this implies that there are still items that can be consumed by the Consumer so there is no need to produce more. Similarly, if free index and full index points to the same index, this implies that there are no item to consume.

ii) Messaging Passing Method

Now, We will start our discussion for the communication between processes via message passing. In this method, processes communicate with each other without using any kind of of shared memory. If two processes p1 and p2 want to communicate with each other, they proceed as follow:

- Establish a communication link (if a link already exists, no need to establish it again.)

- Start exchanging messages using basic primitives.

We need at least two primitives:

- **send**(message, destinaion) or **send**(message)

- **receive**(message, host) or **receive**(message)

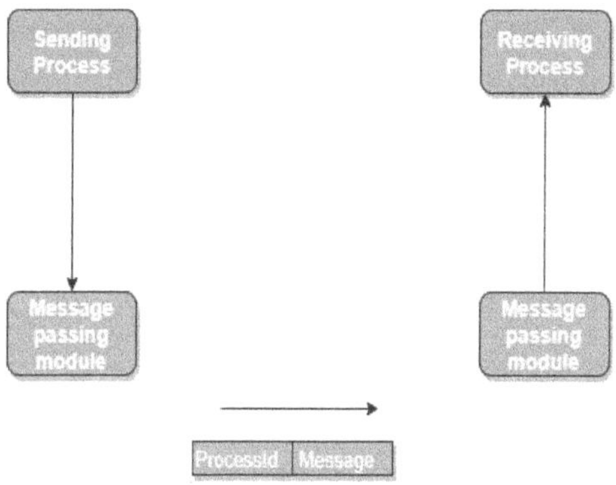

The message size can be of fixed size or of variable size. if it is of fixed size, it is easy for OS designer but complicated for programmer and if it is of variable size then it is easy for programmer but complicated for the OS designer. A standard message can have two parts: **header and body.**

The **header part** is used for storing Message type, destination id, source id, message length and control information. The control information contains information like what to do if runs out of buffer space, sequence number, priority. Generally, message is sent using FIFO style.

Direct and Indirect Communication Link

Now, we will start our discussion about the methods of implementing communication link. While implementing the link, there are some questions which need to be kept in mind like :

1. How are links established?
2. Can a link be associated with more than two processes?
3. How many links can there be between every pair of communicating processes?
4. What is the capacity of a link? Is the size of a message that the link can accommodate fixed or variable?
5. Is a link unidirectional or bi-directional?

A link has some capacity that determines the number of messages that can reside in it temporarily for which Every link has a queue associated with it which can be either of zero capacity or of bounded capacity or of unbounded capacity. In zero capacity, sender wait until receiver inform sender that it has received the message. In non-zero capacity cases, a process does not know whether a message has been received or not after the send operation. For this, the sender must communicate to receiver explicitly. Implementation of the link depends on the situation, it can be either a Direct communication link or an In-directed communication link. **Direct Communication links** are implemented when the processes use specific process identifier for the communication but it is hard to identify the sender ahead of time. **For example: the print server.**

In-directed Communication is done via a shred mailbox (port), which consists of queue of messages. Sender keeps the message in mailbox and receiver picks them up.

Message Passing through Exchanging the Messages

Synchronous and Asynchronous Message Passing

A process that is blocked is one that is waiting for some event, such as a resource becoming available or the completion of an I/O operation. IPC is possible between the processes on same computer as well as on the processes running on different computer i.e. in networked/distributed system. In both cases, the process may or may not be blocked while sending a message or attempting to receive a message so Message passing may be blocking or non-blocking. Blocking is considered **synchronous** and **blocking send** means the sender will be blocked until the message is received by receiver. Similarly, **blocking receive** has the receiver block until a message is available. Non-blocking is considered **asynchronous** and Non-blocking send has the sender sends the message and continue. Similarly, Non-blocking receive has the receiver receive a valid message or null. After a careful analysis, we can come to a conclusion that, for a sender it is more natural to be non-blocking after message passing as there may be a need to send the message to different processes But the sender expect acknowledgement from receiver in case the send fails. Similarly, it is more natural for a receiver to be blocking after issuing the receive as the information from the received message may be used for further execution but at the same time, if the message send keep on failing, receiver will have to wait for indefinitely. That is why we also consider the other possibility of message passing. There are basically three most preferred combinations:

- Blocking send and blocking receive
- Non-blocking send and Non-blocking receive
- Non-blocking send and Blocking receive (Mostly used)

In Direct message passing, The process which want to communicate must explicitly name the recipient or sender of communication. e.g. **send(p1, message)** means send the message to p1. Similarly, **receive (p2, message)** means receive the message from p2.

In this method of communication, the communication link get established automatically, which can be either unidirectional or bidirectional, but one link can be used between one pair of the sender and receiver and one pair of sender and receiver should not possess more than one pair of link. Symmetry and asymmetry between the sending and receiving can also be implemented i.e. either both process will name each other for sending and receiving the messages or only sender will name receiver for sending the message and there is no need for receiver for naming the sender for receiving the message. The problem with this method of communication is that if the name of one process changes, this method will not work.

In Indirect message passing, processes uses mailboxes (also referred to as ports) for sending and receiving messages. Each mailbox has a unique id and processes can communicate only if they share a mailbox. Link established only if processes share a common mailbox and a single link can be associated with many processes. Each pair of processes can share several communication links and these link may be unidirectional or bi-directional. Suppose two process want to communicate though Indirect message passing, the required operations are: create a mail box, use this mail box for sending and receiving messages, destroy the mail box. The standard primitives used are: **send(A, message)** which means send the message to mailbox A. The primitive for the receiving the message also works in the same way e.g. **received (A, message)**. There is a problem in this mailbox implementation. Suppose there are more than two processes sharing the same mailbox and suppose the process p1 sends a message to the mailbox, which process will be the receiver? This can be solved by either forcing that only two processes can share a single mailbox or enforcing that only one process is allowed to execute the receive at a given time or select any process randomly and notify the sender about the receiver. A mailbox can be made private to a single sender/receiver pair and can also be shared between multiple sender/receiver pairs. Port is an implementation of such mailbox which can have multiple sender and single receiver. It is used in client/server application (Here server is the receiver). The port is owned by the receiving process and created by OS on the request of the receiver process and can be destroyed either on request of the same receiver process or when the receiver terminates itself. Enforcing that only one process is allowed to execute the receive can be done using the concept of mutual exclusion. **Mutex mailbox** is create which is shared by n process. Sender is non-blocking and sends the message. The first process which executes the receive will enter in the critical section and all other processes will be blocking and will wait.

Now, lets discuss the Producer-Consumer problem using message passing concept. The producer place items (inside messages) in the mailbox and the consumer can consume item when at least one message present in the mailbox. The code are given below:

Producer Code

```
void Producer(void){
int item;
Message m;
while(1){
receive(Consumer, &m);
item = produce();
build_message(&m , item ) ;
send(Consumer, &m);
}
}
```

Consumer Code

```
void Consumer(void){
int item;
Message m;
while(1){
receive(Producer, &m);
item = extracted_item();
send(Producer, &m);
consume_item(item);
}
}
```

Examples of IPC Systems

1. Posix : uses shared memory method.
2. Mach : uses message passing
3. Windows XP : uses message passing using local procedural calls

Communication in Client/Server Architecture

There are various mechanism:

- Pipe
- Socket
- Remote Procedural calls (RPCs)

The above three methods will be discussed later article as all of them are quite conceptual and deserve their own separate articles.

References

1. Operating System Concepts by Galvin et al.
2. Lecture notes/ppt of Ariel J. Frank, Bar-Ilan University

5.2. Task Synchronization/ Communication

One of the most useful developments in the history of computing is multitasking and multithreading. This technique isn't always available to an embedded system engineer, but some embedded systems and RTOS have multithreading (MT) capability. The chapters in this section will talk about some of the uses of MT, and will discuss some of the common pitfalls associated with MT programming. This page is only going to serve as a brief reference to multi-threaded programming.

Preemptive Multithreading

When the first multi-tasking systems were established, they did not have a central controller. Multi-tasking was established by having programs voluntarily give up control to the system, and the system would then give control to another process. This system worked reasonably well, except that any program that was misbehaving would slow down the entire system. For instance, if a program got stuck in an infinite loop, it would never give up control, and the system would freeze.

The solution to this problem is **preemptive multithreading**. In a preemptive environment, control could be moved from one process to another process at any given time. The process that was "preempted" would not even know that anything had happened, except maybe there would be a larger than average delay between 2 instructions. Preemptive multithreading allows for programs that do not voluntarily give up control, and it also allows a computer to continue functioning when a single process hangs.

There are a number of problems associated with preemptive multithreading that all stem from the fact that control is taken away from one process when it is not necessarily prepared to give up control. For instance, if one process were writing to a memory location, and was preempted, the next process would see half-written data, or even corrupted data in that memory location. Or, if a task was reading in data from an input port, and it was preempted, the timing would be wrong, and data would be missed from the line. Clearly, this is unacceptable.

The solution to this new problem then is the idea of synchronization. Synchronization is a series of tools provided by the preemptive multithreaded operating system to ensure that these problems are avoided. Synchronization tools can include timers, "critical sections," and locks. Timers can ensure that a given process may be preempted, but only for a certain time. Critical sections are commands in the code that prevent the system from switching control for a certain time. Locks are commands that prevent interference in atomic operations. These topics will all be discussed in the following chapters.

Mutexes

The term **Mutex** is short for "Mutual Exclusion", and is a type of mechanism used in a preemptive environment that can prevent unauthorized access to resources that are currently in use. Mutexes follow several rules:

1. Mutexes are system wide objects, that are maintained by the kernel.
2. Mutexes can only be owned by one process at a time
3. Mutexes can be acquired by asking the kernel to allocate that mutex to the current task
4. If a Mutex is already allocated, the request function will block until the mutex is available.

In general, it is considered good programming practice to release mutexes as quickly as possible. Some problems with mutexes will be discussed in the chapter on deadlocks.

Spin Locks

Spin locks is a quick form of synchronization methods. It is named after its behavior - spin in the loop while the condition is false. To implement spin lock system should support test-and-set idiom or give exclusive access to a locking thread by any means (masking interrupts, locking bus).

An advantage of spin locks is that they are very simple. A disadvantage is that they waste CPU cycles in loop waiting. Most common use of spin locks is to synchronize quick access to objects. It is not advisable to do a long computations while spin locked a section.

Sentinels/ Critical Sections

A critical section is a sequence of computer instructions that may malfunction if interrupted. An atomic operation is a sequence of computer instructions that cannot be interrupted and function correctly. In practice, these two subtly different definitions are often combined. Operating systems provide synchronization objects to meet these requirements, and some actually call these objects as "critical sections," "atomic operations" or "monitors."

An example of a critical section is code that removes data from a queue that is filled by an interrupt. If the critical section is not protected, the interrupt can occur while the dequeuing function is changing pointers, and corrupt the queue pointers. An example of an atomic operation is an I/O read where the process must read all the data at a particular rate, and cannot be preempted while reading.

A generally good programming practice is to have programs exit their critical sections as quickly as possible, because holding a critical section for too long will cause other processes on the system not to get any time, and will cause a major performance decrease. Critical sections should be used with care.

Dead Lock

A **deadlock** occurs when a series of synchronization objects are held in a preemptive MT system in such a way that no process can move forward. Let us take a look at an example:

Let's say that we have 2 threads: T1 and T2. We also have 2 mutexes, M1 and M2.

1. T1 asks for and acquires mutex M1.
2. T2 acquires M2
3. T1 asks for M2, and the system transfers control to T2 until T2 releases M2.
4. T2 asks for M1, and the system is in deadlock (neither thread can continue until the other releases it's mutex).

This is a very difficult problem to diagnose, and an even more difficult problem to fix. This chapter will provide some general guide-lines for preventing deadlocks.

Device and Drives

- Defining device drivers
- Discussing the difference between architecture-specific and board-specific drivers
- Providing several examples of different types of device drivers

Most embedded hardware requires some type of software initialization and management. The software that directly interfaces with and controls this hardware is called a device driver.

All embedded systems that require software have, at the very least, device driver software in their system software layer. Device drivers are the software libraries that initialize the hardware and manage access to the hardware by higher layers of software. Device drivers are the liaison between the hardware and the operating system, middleware, and application layers. (See Figure 5.2.)

The reader must always check the details about the particular hardware if the hardware component is not 100% identical to what is currently supported by the embedded system. Never assume existing device drivers in the embedded system will be compatible for a particular hardware part—even if the hardware is the same type of hardware that the embedded device currently supports! So, it is very important when trying to understand device driver libraries that:

- Different types of hardware will have different device driver requirements that need to be met.
- Even the same type of hardware, such as Flash memory, that are created by different manufacturers can require substantially different device driver software libraries to support within the embedded device.

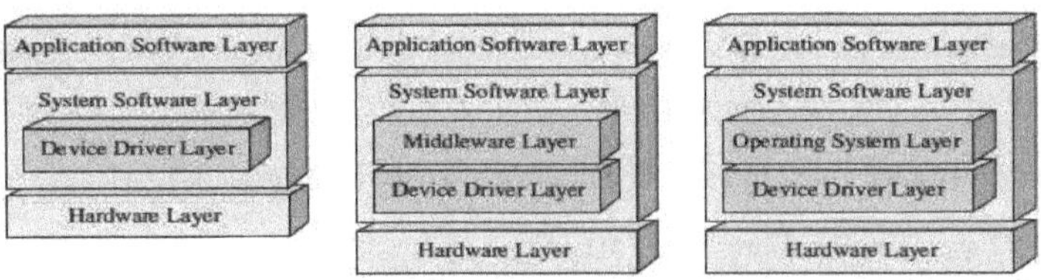

Figure 5.2: Embedded Systems Model and Device Drivers

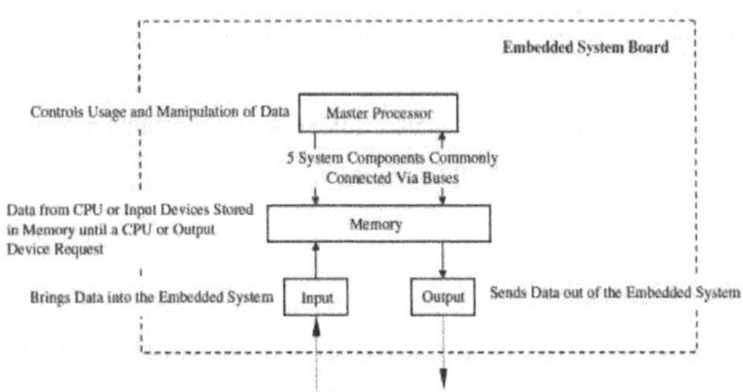

Figure 5.3: Embedded System Board Organization.[1]. Based Upon the Von Neumann Architecture Model (Also Referred to as the Princeton Architecture)

The types of hardware components needing the support of device drivers vary from board to board, but they can be categorized according to the von Neumann model approach introduced in Chapter 3 (see Figure 5.3).

The von Neumann model can be used as a software model as well as a hardware model in determining what device drivers are required within a particular platform. Specifically, this can include drivers for the master processor architecture-specific functionality, memory and memory management drivers, bus initialization and transaction drivers, and I/O (input/output) initialization and control drivers (such as for networking, graphics, input devices, storage devices, or debugging I/O) both at the board and master CPU level.

Device drivers are typically considered either architecture-specific or generic. A device driver that is architecture-specific manages the hardware that is integrated into the master processor (the architecture).

Examples of architecture-specific drivers that initialize and enable components within a master processor include on-chip memory, integrated memory managers (memory management units (MMUs)), and floating-point hardware. A device driver that is generic manages hardware that is located on the board and not integrated onto the master processor.

In a generic driver, there are typically architecture-specific portions of source code, because the master processor is the central control unit and to gain access to anything on the board usually means going through the master processor. However, the generic driver also manages board hardware that is not specific to that particular processor, which means that a generic driver can be configured to run on a variety of architectures that contain the related board hardware for which the driver is written. Generic drivers include code that initializes and manages access to the remaining major components of the board, including board buses (I2C, PCI, PCMCIA, etc.), off-chip memory (controllers, level 2+ cache, Flash, etc.), and off-chip I/O (Ethernet, **RS-232**, display, mouse, etc.).

5.3. How to choose an RTOS?

7 Characteristics to Consider when Selecting an RTOS

Selecting the right RTOS is a critical step in any embedded software development project. Selecting the wrong RTOS could affect project costs, time to market and have real-time implications on the behavior of the system.

When selecting an RTOS, teams usually focus just on cost but there are seven characteristics that should be considered. Let's examine each one.

Characteristic #1 – Performance

RTOS performance is a critical factor to consider when selecting an RTOS. All RTOSes are NOT created equal and an attempt to save a few dollars can cost orders of magnitude more. When it comes to performance, developers have a variety of factors that need to be considered. First, memory requirements such as ROM, flash and RAM footprints need to be considered. RTOSes are powerful and with that power comes additional code and data needs. Second, processing speed such as interrupt latency and context switch times should be reviewed. A high quality RTOS will document these parameters for a variety of architectures and clock speeds.

Characteristic #2 – Features

Every RTOS doesn't have the exact same features or the features implemented in the most optimal manner. Developers need to evaluate which features are the most critical to the systems success and select an RTOS that has those features. Developers may want to consider scalability, safety certifications or even the efficiency of memory protection schemes. A little thought about feature is whether the RTOS conforms to standard interfaces such as POSIX. Even the way in which RTOS tasks and objects are allocated could be an important feature. Many RTOSes use dynamic memory allocation for tasks which for resource constrained embedded system could be dangerous due to heap fragmentation and other issues. An RTOS that can statically allocate tasks might be the better choice.

Characteristic #3 – Cost

Undoubtedly one of the largest, if not only thought about RTOS characteristic is cost. Despite the huge efforts required in labor to develop robust software, no one wants to pay for it! Developers need to get over it and probably evaluate what an RTOS may really cost. A few considerations for commercial RTOSes are the upfront costs for licensing and any recurring licenses such as royalties. In additional to these obvious costs, developers need to also consider the total cost of ownership for the RTOS. That is, the cost to learn, setup, integrate and debug the selected operating system. Total cost of ownership for an open source RTOS can potentially exceed that of a commercially purchased RTOS due to lack of support, poor code quality and so forth.

Characteristic #4 – Ecosystem

Having the best performance, features and cost doesn't mean a thing if there isn't a large and vibrant community to support the RTOS. A software products ecosystem is a critical piece of the selection process in order to ensure ease of integration, support and product lifetime. When developers investigate an RTOS ecosystem, they should determine whether the RTOS is supported and adopted by their industry and the embedded software industry as a whole. They should determine whether there is support for a variety of architectures and processors or whether the RTOS is just a one trick pony. The availability of numerous examples and ports is also an important indicator that the RTOS is supported and has a strong community of users around it.

Characteristic #5 – Middleware

Many RTOSes come with middleware components or have third parties who have developed components that integrate into the RTOS. Developers should evaluate their RTOSes middleware and determine what the integration effort might be. Sometimes the integration is seamless while other times it is an obvious nightmare. Some RTOSes lack support for middleware and open source components need to be integrated which can lead to a variety of time consuming integration issues. Verify that the middleware has common components such as USB, TCP/IP, file systems and graphics generators before jumping in with both feet.

Characteristic #6 – Vendor

Take a good hard look at the vendor who developed, maintains and distributes the RTOS. Do they have a good track record dating back at least five, ten or fifteen years? Examine their source code and documentation.

A good supplier with have meticulous documentation that answers many of the questions that would arise while integrating the RTOS into the system. No matter how good documentation gets, it will never be perfect. Testing how fast the vendor is to respond to question and support issues could be critical and save precious time and money getting the product out the door. Don't just blindly trust. Be an engineer and put the vendor to the test and see if they squirm or roll up their sleeves.

Characteristic #7 – Engineering Team

The characteristic of RTOS selection that is probably the most common to overlook is the engineering team. The RTOS that is selected should minimize the labor intensity for the team and allow them to focus on product differentiators rather than increase it as they learn how to integrate and setup an RTOS. As much as we like to grow professionally as engineers, we should attempt to select an RTOS we are familiar with and can work most efficiently with. Sometimes development doesn't work out that way but we should at least try.

Conclusions

Performance, features, cost, ecosystem, middleware, vendor and the engineering team are just examples of characteristics that should be evaluated when a development team is ready to select an RTOS for their product.

As engineers we need to make sure we set aside our own biases and make decisions based on the facts. For developers interested in a method to perform an unbiased selection of an RTOS, download my RTOS Selection Matrix and read my DesignNews article "7 Steps to select the right RTOS".

Given the definition of embedded systems presented earlier in this chapter, the first such systems could not possibly have appeared before 1971. That was the year Intel introduced the world's first single-chip microprocessor.

This chip, the 4004, was designed for use in a line of business calculators produced by the Japanese company Busicom. In 1969, Busicom asked Intel to design a set of custom integrated circuits, one for each of its new calculator models.

The 4004 was Intel's response. Rather than design custom hardware for each calculator, Intel proposed a general-purpose circuit that could be used throughout the entire line of calculators.

This general-purpose processor was designed to read and execute a set of instructions—software—stored in an external memory chip. Intel's idea was that the software would give each calculator its unique set of features and that this design style would drive demand for its core business in memory chips.

The microprocessor was an overnight success, and its use increased steadily over the next decade. Early embedded applications included unmanned space probes, computerized traffic lights, and aircraft flight control systems. In the 1980s and 1990s, embedded systems quietly rode the waves of the microcomputer age and brought microprocessors into every part of our personal and professional lives. Most of the electronic devices in our kitchens (bread machines, food processors, and microwave ovens), living rooms (televisions, stereos, and remote controls), and workplaces (fax machines, pagers, laser printers, cash registers, and credit card readers) are embedded systems; over 6 billion new microprocessors are used each year. Less than 2 percent (or about 100 million per year) of these microprocessors are used in general-purpose computers.

It seems inevitable that the number of embedded systems will continue to increase rapidly. Already there are promising new embedded devices that have enormous market potential: light switches and thermostats that are networked together and can be controlled wirelessly by a central computer, intelligent air-bag systems that don't inflate when children or small adults are present, medical monitoring devices that can notify a doctor if a patient's physiological conditions are at critical levels, and dashboard navigation systems that inform you of the best route to your destination under current traffic conditions. Clearly, individuals who possess the skills and the desire to design the next generation of embedded systems will be in demand for quite some time.

Real-Time Systems

One subclass of embedded systems deserves an introduction at this point. A *real-time system* has timing constraints.

The function of a real-time system is thus partly specified in terms of its ability to make certain calculations or decisions in a timely manner. These important calculations or activities have deadlines for completion.

The crucial distinction among real-time systems lies in what happens if a deadline is missed. For example, if the real-time system is part of an airplane's flight control system, the lives of the passengers and crew may be endangered by a single missed deadline. However, if instead the system is involved in satellite communication, the damage could be limited to a single corrupt data packet (which may or may not have catastrophic consequences depending on the application and error recovery scheme).

The more severe the consequences, the more likely it will be said that the deadline is "hard" and thus, that the system is a *hard real-time system*. Real-time systems at the other end of this continuum are said to have "soft" deadlines—a *soft real-time system*. Shows some examples of hard and soft real-time systems.

Real-time system design is not simply about speed. Deadlines for real-time systems vary; one deadline might be in a millisecond, while another is an hour away. The main concern for a real-time system is that there is a guarantee that the hard deadlines of the system are always met. In order to accomplish this the system must be predictable.

The architecture of the embedded software, and its interaction with the system hardware, play a key role in ensuring that real-time systems meet their deadlines. Key software design issues include whether polling is sufficient or interrupts should be used, and what priorities should be assigned to the various tasks and interrupts. Additional forethought must go into understanding the worst-case performance requirements of the specific system activities.

All of the topics and examples presented in this book are applicable to the designers of real-time systems. The designer of a real-time system must be more diligent in his work. He must guarantee reliable operation of the software and hardware under all possible conditions. And, to the degree that human lives depend upon the system's proper execution, this guarantee must be backed by engineering calculations and descriptive paperwork.

Variations on a Theme

Unlike software designed for general-purpose computers, embedded software cannot usually be run on other embedded systems without significant modification. This is mainly because of the incredible variety of hardware in use in embedded systems. The hardware in each embedded system is tailored specifically to the application, in order to keep system costs low. As a result, unnecessary circuitry is eliminated and hardware resources are shared wherever possible.

In this section, you will learn which hardware features are common across all embedded systems and why there is so much variation with respect to just about everything else. Later in the book, we will look at some techniques that can be used to minimize the impact of software changes so they are not needed throughout all layers of the software.

Common System Components

By definition, all embedded systems contain a processor and software, but what other features do they have in common? Certainly, in order to have software, there must be a place to store the executable code and temporary storage for runtime data manipulation. These take the form of *read-only memory* (ROM) and *random access memory* (RAM), respectively; most embedded systems have some of each. If only a small amount of memory is required, it might be contained within the same chip as the processor. Otherwise, one or both types of memory reside in external memory chips.

All embedded systems also contain some type of inputs and outputs. For example, in a microwave oven, the inputs are the buttons on the front panel and a temperature probe, and the outputs are the human-readable display and the microwave radiation. The outputs of the embedded system are almost always a function of its inputs and several other factors (elapsed time, current temperature, etc.). The inputs to the system usually take the form of sensors and probes, communication signals, or control knobs and buttons. The outputs are typically displays, communication signals, or changes to the physical world. See Figure 1-2 for a general example of an embedded system.

A generic Embedded System

With the exception of these few common features, the rest of the embedded hardware is usually unique and, therefore, requires unique software. This variation is the result of many competing design criteria.

The software for the generic embedded system shown in Figure 1-2 varies depending on the functionality needed. The hardware is the blank canvas, and the software is the paint that we add in order to make the picture come to life. Figure 1-3 gives just a couple of possible high-level diagrams that could be implemented on such a generic embedded system.

The device drivers are embedded software modules that contain the functionality to operate the individual hardware devices. The reason for the device driver software is to remove the need for the application to know how to control each piece of hardware. Each individual device driver would typically need to know only how to control its hardware device. For instance, for a microwave oven, separate device drivers control the keypad, display, temperature probe, and radiation control.

If more functionality is required, it is sometimes necessary to include additional layers in the embedded software to assist with this added functionality. In this example, the complex diagram includes a *real-time operating system* (*RTOS*) and a networking stack. The RTOS can help the programmer separate the application's functionality into distinct tasks for better organization of the application software and a more responsive system. We will investigate the use of an RTOS later in this book. The network stack also adds to the functionality of the basic embedded system; a microwave oven might use it to pop up a message on your desktop computer when your lunch is ready.

The responsibilities of the application software layer is the same in both the basic and the complex embedded software diagrams. In a microwave oven, the application processes the different inputs and controls the outputs based on what the user commands it to do.

You'll notice that the software in Figure 1-3 is represented by discrete blocks stacked on top of one another with fixed borders. This is done deliberately, to indicate the separation of the different software functional layers that make up the complete embedded software system. Later, we will break down these blocks further to show you how you can keep your embedded software clean, easy to read, and portable. Keeping these software layers distinct, with well-defined methods that neighboring layers can use to communicate, helps you write good embedded software.

Requirements That Affect Design Choices

Each embedded system must meet a completely different set of requirements, any or all of which can affect the compromises and trade-offs made during the development of the product. For example, if the system must have a production cost of less than $10, other desirable traits—such as processing power and system reliability—might need to be sacrificed in order to meet that goal.

Of course, production cost is only one of the possible constraints under which embedded hardware designers work. Other common design requirements include:

Processing Power

The workload that the main chip can handle. A common way to compare processing power is the *millions of instructions per second* (MIPS) rating. If two otherwise similar processors have ratings of 25 MIPS and 40 MIPS, the latter is said to be the more powerful. However, other important features of the processor need to be considered. One is the register width, which typically ranges from 8 to 64 bits. Today's general-purpose computers use 32- and 64-bit processors exclusively, but embedded systems are still mainly built with less costly 4-, 8-, and 16-bit processors.

Memory

The amount of memory (ROM and RAM) required to hold the executable software and the data it manipulates. Here the hardware designer must usually make his best estimate up front and be prepared to increase or decrease the actual amount as the software is being developed. The amount of memory required can also affect the processor selection. In general, the register width of a processor establishes the upper limit of the amount of memory it can access (e.g., a 16-bit address register can address only 64 KB (2^{16}) memory locations). [1]

Number of Units

The expected production run. The trade-off between production cost and development cost is affected most by the number of units expected to be produced and sold. For example, it rarely makes sense to develop custom hardware components for a low-volume product.

Power Consumption

The amount of power used during operation. This is extremely important, especially for battery-powered portable devices. A common metric used to compare the power requirements of portable devices is mW/MIPS (milliwatts per MIPS); the greater this value, the more power is required to get work done. Lower power consumption can also lead to other favorable device characteristics, such as less heat, smaller batteries, less weight, smaller size, and simpler mechanical design.

Development Cost

The cost of the hardware and software design processes, known as *nonrecurring engineering* (NRE). This is a fixed, one-time cost, so on some projects, money is no object (usually for high-volume products), whereas on other projects, this is the only accurate measure of system cost (for the production of a small number of units).

Lifetime

How long the product is expected to stay in use. The required or expected lifetime affects all sorts of design decisions, from the selection of hardware components to how much system development and production is allowed to cost. How long must the system continue to function (on average)? A month, a year, or a decade?

Reliability

How reliable the final product must be. If it is a children's toy, it may not have to work properly 100 percent of the time, but if it's an antilock braking system for a car, it had sure better do what it is supposed to do each and every time.

In addition to these general requirements, each system has detailed functional requirements. These are the things that give the embedded system its unique identity as a microwave oven, pacemaker, or pager.

Table 5.1 illustrates the range of typical values for each of the previous design requirements. The "low," "medium," and "high" labels are meant for illustration purposes and should not be taken as strict delineations. An actual product has one selection from each row. In some cases, two or more of the criteria are linked. For example, increases in required processing power could lead to increased production costs. Conversely, we might imagine that the same increase in processing power would have the effect of decreasing the development costs—by reducing the complexity of the hardware and software design. So the values in a particular column do not necessarily go together.

Table 5.1: Common Design Requirements for Embedded Systems

Criterion	Low	Medium	High
Processor	4- or 8-bit	16-bit	32- or 64-bit
Memory	< 64 KB	64 KB to 1 MB	> 1 MB
Development cost	< $100,000	$100,000 to $1,000,000	> $1,000,000
Production cost	< $10	$10 to $1,000	> $1,000
Number of units	< 100	100 to 10,000	> 10,000
Power consumption	> 10 mW/MIPS	1 to 10 mW/MIPS	< 1 mW/MIPS
Lifetime	Days, weeks, or months	Years	Decades
Reliability	May occasionally fail	Must work reliably	Must be fail-proof

Embedded Design Examples

To demonstrate the variation in design requirements from one embedded system to the next, as well as the possible effects of these requirements on the hardware, we will now take some time to describe three embedded systems in some detail. Our goal is to put you in the system designer's shoes for a few moments before narrowing our discussion to embedded software development.

Digital Watch

At the current peak of the evolutionary path that began with sundials, water clocks, and hourglasses is the digital watch. Among its many features are the presentation of the date and time (usually to the nearest second), the measurement of the length of an event to the nearest hundredth of a second, and the generation of an annoying little sound at the beginning of each hour. As it turns out, these are very simple tasks that do not require very much processing power or memory. In fact, the only reason to employ a processor at all is to support a range of models and features from a single hardware design.

The typical digital watch contains a simple, inexpensive 4-bit processor. Because processors with such small registers cannot address very much memory, this type of processor usually contains its own on-chip ROM. And, if there are sufficient registers available, this application may not require any RAM at all. In fact, all of the electronics— processor, memory, counters, and real-time clocks—are likely to be stored in a single chip. The only other hardware elements of the watch are the inputs (buttons) and outputs (display and speaker).

A digital watch designer's goal is to create a reasonably reliable product that has an extraordinarily low production cost. If, after production, some watches are found to keep more reliable time than most, they can be sold under a brand name with a higher markup. For the rest, a profit can still be made by selling the watch through a discount sales channel. For lower-cost versions, the stopwatch buttons or speaker could be eliminated. This would limit the functionality of the watch but might require few or even no software changes. And, of course, the cost of all this development effort may be fairly high, because it will be amortized over hundreds of thousands or even millions of watch sales.

In the case of the digital watch, we see that software, especially when carefully designed, allows enormous flexibility in response to a rapidly changing and highly competitive market.

Video Game Player

When you pull the Sony PlayStation 2 out from your entertainment center, you are preparing to use an embedded system. In some cases, these machines are more powerful than personal computers of the same generation. Yet video game players for the home market are relatively inexpensive compared with personal computers. It is the competing requirements of high processing power and low production cost that keep video game designers awake at night.

The companies that produce video game players don't usually care how much it costs to develop the system as long as the production costs of the resulting product are low—typically around a hundred dollars. They might even encourage their engineers to design custom processors at a development cost of millions of dollars each. So, although there might be a 64-bit processor inside your video game player, it is probably not the same processor that would be found in a general-purpose computer. In all likelihood, the processor is highly specialized for the demands of the video games it is intended to play.

Because production cost is so crucial in the home video game market, the designers also use tricks to shift the costs around. For example, one tactic is to move as much of the memory and other peripheral electronics as possible off of the main circuit board and onto the game cartridges. [2] This helps to reduce the cost of the game player but increases the price of every game. So, while the system might have a powerful 64-bit processor, it might have only a few megabytes of memory on the main circuit board. This is just enough memory to bootstrap the machine to a state from which it can access additional memory on the game cartridge.

We can see from the case of the video game player that in high-volume products, a lot of development effort can be sunk into fine-tuning every aspect of a product.

Mars Rover

In 1976, two unmanned spacecrafts arrived on the planet Mars. As part of their mission, they were to collect samples of the Martian surface, analyze the chemical makeup of each, and transmit the results to scientists back on Earth.

Those Viking missions were amazing. Surrounded by personal computers that must be rebooted occasionally, we might find it remarkable that more than 30 years ago, a team of scientists and engineers successfully built two computers that survived a journey of 34 million miles and functioned correctly for half a decade. Clearly, reliability was one of the most important requirements for these systems.

What if a memory chip had failed? Or the software had contained bugs that had caused it to crash? Or an electrical connection had broken during impact? There is no way to prevent such problems from occurring, and on other space missions, these problems have proved ruinous. So, all of these potential failure points and many others had to be eliminated by adding redundant circuitry or extra functionality: an extra processor here, special memory diagnostics there, a hardware timer to reset the system if the software got stuck, and so on.

More recently, NASA launched the Pathfinder mission. Its primary goal was to demonstrate the feasibility of getting to Mars on a budget. Of course, given the advances in technology made since the mid-70s, the designers didn't have to give up too much to accomplish this. They might have reduced the amount of redundancy somewhat, but they still gave Pathfinder more processing power and memory than Viking. The Mars Pathfinder was actually two embedded systems: a landing craft and a rover.

The landing craft had a 32-bit processor and 128 MB of RAM; the rover, on the other hand, had only an 8-bit processor and 512 KB of RAM. These choices reflect the different functional requirements of the two systems.

Production cost probably wasn't much of an issue in either case; any investment would have been worth an improved likelihood of success.

Life as an Embedded Software Developer

Let's now take a brief look at some of the qualities of embedded software that set embedded developers apart from other types of software developers. An embedded software developer is the one who gets her hands dirty by getting down close to the hardware.

Embedded software development, in most cases, requires close interaction with the physical world—the hardware platform. We say "in most cases" because there are very large embedded systems that require individuals to work solely on the application-layer software for the system. These application developers typically do not have any interaction with the hardware. When designed properly, the hardware device drivers are abstracted away from the actual hardware so that a developer writing software at the application level doesn't know how a string gets output to the display, just that it happens when a particular routine is called with the proper parameters.

Hardware Knowledge

The embedded software developer must become intimately familiar with the integrated circuits, the boards and buses, and the attached devices used in order to write solid embedded software (also called *firmware*). Embedded developers shouldn't be afraid to dive into the schematics, grab an oscilloscope probe, and start poking around the circuit to find out what is going on.

Efficient Code

Because embedded systems are typically designed with the least powerful and most cost-effective processor that meets the performance requirements of the system, embedded software developers must make every line of code count. The ability to write efficient code is a great quality to possess as a firmware developer.

Peripheral Interfaces

At the lowest level, firmware is very specialized, because each component or circuit has its own activity to perform and, furthermore, its own way of performing that activity. Embedded developers need to know how to communicate with the different devices or *peripherals* in order to have full control of the devices in the system. Reacting to stimuli from external peripherals is a large part of embedded software development.

For example, in one microwave oven, the firmware might get the data from a temperature sensor by reading an 8-bit register in an external analog-to-digital converter; in another system, the data might be extracted by controlling a serial bus that interfaces to the external sensor circuit via a single wire.

Robust Code

There are expectations that embedded systems will run for years in most cases. This is not a typical requirement for software applications written for a PC or Mac. Now, there are exceptions. However, if you had to keep unplugging your microwave in order to get it to heat up your lunch for the proper amount of time, it would probably be the last time you purchased a product from that company.

Minimal Resources

Along the same lines of creating a more robust system, another large differentiator between embedded software and other types of software is resource constraints. The rules for writing firmware are different from the rules for writing software for a PC. Take memory allocation, for instance.

An application for a modern PC can take for granted that it will have access to practically limitless resources. But in an embedded system, you will run out of memory if you do not plan ahead and design the software properly.

An embedded software developer must closely manage resources, from memory to processing power, so that the system operates up to specification and so failures don't occur. For example, using standard dynamic memory allocation functions can cause fragmentation, and eventually the system may cease to operate. This requires a reboot since you have no place to store incoming data.

Quite often, in embedded software, a developer will allocate all memory needed by the system at initialization time. This is safer than using dynamic memory allocation, though it cannot always be done.

Reusable Software

As we mentioned before, *code portability* or *code reuse*—writing software so that it can be moved from hardware platform to hardware platform—is very useful to aid transition to new projects.

This cannot always be done; we have seen how individual each embedded system is. Throughout this book, we will look at basic methods to ensure that your embedded code can be moved more easily from project to project.

Development Tools

The tools you will use throughout your career as an embedded developer will vary from company to company and often from project to project. This means you will need to learn new tools as you continue in your career. Typically, these tools are not as powerful or as easy to use as those used in PC software development.

The debugging tools you might come across could vary from a simple LED to a full-blown *in-circuit emulator* (ICE). This requires you, as the firmware developer, and the one responsible for debugging your code, to be very resourceful and have a bag of techniques you can call upon when the debug environment is lacking. Throughout the book, we will present different "low-level software tools" you can implement with little impact on the hardware design.

These are just a few qualities that separate embedded software developers from the rest of the pack. We will investigate these and other techniques that are specific to embedded software development as we continue.

5.4. The C Language: The Lowest Common Denominator

One of the few constants across most embedded systems is the use of the C programming language. More than any other, C has become the language of embedded programmers. This has not always been the case, and it will not continue to be so forever. However, at this time, C is the closest thing there is to a standard in the embedded world. In this section, we'll explain why C has become so popular and why we have chosen it as the primary language of this book.

Because successful software development so frequently depends on selecting the best language for a given project, it is surprising to find that one language has proven itself appropriate for both 8-bit and 64-bit processors; in systems with bytes, kilobytes, and megabytes of memory; and for development teams that range from one to a dozen or more people. Yet this is precisely the range of projects in which C has thrived.

The C programming language has plenty of advantages. It is small and fairly simple to learn, compilers are available for almost every processor in use today, and there is a very large body of experienced C programmers. In addition, C has the benefit of processor-independence, which allows programmers to concentrate on algorithms and applications rather than on the details of a particular processor architecture. However, many of these advantages apply equally to other high-level languages. So why has C succeeded where so many other languages have largely failed?

Perhaps the greatest strength of C—and the thing that sets it apart from languages such as Pascal and FORTRAN—is that it is a very "low-level" high-level language. As we shall see throughout the book, C gives embedded programmers an extraordinary degree of direct hardware control without sacrificing the benefits of high-level languages. The "low-level" nature of C was a clear intention of the language's creators. In fact, Brian W. Kernighan and Dennis M. Ritchie included the following comment in the opening pages of their book *The C Programming Language* (Prentice Hall).

C is a relatively "low level" language. This characterization is not pejorative; it simply means that C deals with the same sort of objects that most computers do. These may be combined and moved about with the arithmetic and logical operators implemented by real machines.

Few popular high-level languages can compete with C in the production of compact, efficient code for almost all processors. And, of these, only C allows programmers to interact with the underlying hardware so easily.

Other Embedded Languages

Of course, C is not the only language used by embedded programmers. At least four other languages—assembly, C++, Forth, and Ada—are worth mentioning in greater detail.

In the early days, embedded software was written exclusively in the assembly language of the target processor. This gave programmers complete control of the processor and other hardware, but at a price. Assembly languages have many disadvantages, not the least of which are higher software development costs and a lack of code portability. In addition, finding skilled assembly programmers has become much more difficult in recent years. Assembly is now used primarily as an adjunct to the high-level language, usually only for startup system code or those small pieces of code that must be extremely efficient or ultra-compact, or cannot be written in any other way.

Forth is efficient but extremely low-level and unusual; learning to get work done with it takes more time than with C.

C++ is an object-oriented superset of C that is increasingly popular among embedded programmers. All of the core language features are the same as C, but C++ adds new functionality for better data abstraction and a more object-oriented style of programming. These new features are very helpful to software developers, but some of them reduce the efficiency of the executable program. So C++ tends to be most popular with large development teams, where the benefits to developers outweigh the loss of program efficiency.

Ada is also an object-oriented language, though substantially different from C++. Ada was originally designed by the U.S. Department of Defense for the development of mission-critical military software. Despite being twice accepted as an international standard (Ada83 and Ada95), it has not gained much of a foothold outside of the defense and aerospace industries. And it has been losing ground there in recent years. This is unfortunate because the Ada language has many features that would simplify embedded software development if used instead of C or C++.

Choosing a Language for the Book

A major question facing the authors of a book such as this one is which programming language or languages to discuss. Attempting to cover too many languages might confuse the reader or detract from more important points. On the other hand, focusing too narrowly could make the discussion unnecessarily academic or (worse for the authors and publisher) limit the potential market for the book.

Certainly, C must be the centerpiece of any book about embedded programming, and this book is no exception. All of the sample code is written in C, and the discussion will focus on C-related programming issues. Of course, everything that is said about C programming applies equally to C++. We will use assembly language only when a particular programming task cannot be accomplished in any other way.

We feel that this focus on C with a brief introduction to assembly most accurately reflects the way embedded software is actually developed today and the way it will continue to be developed in the near term. This is why examples in this edition do not use C++. We hope that this choice will keep the discussion clear, provide information that is useful to people developing actual systems, and include as large a potential audience as possible.